BREAKING OUT of SHOW BUSINESS

★ ★★★ ★

★★★ *What I've* ★★★
Discovered
★★ *by Not Being* ★★
Discovered

A POST HILL PRESS book

ISBN (Trade Paperback): 978-1-61868-921-4
ISBN (eBook): 978-1-61868-922-1

Post Hill
PRESS

Special thanks to:

Nick Buzzell at NBTV for thinking enough of me to approach and ask me to write this.

Post Hill Press for partnering in this walk down memory lane, minus all the libel shit I would have loved to have put in.

My new friend, Steve Bruner, for helping me balance writing the way I speak without crucifying English grammar to the point of being deported. You are as intelligent as you are funny.

Jake Strasser, friends and family, and all those during this huge, lifelong education with whom I have crossed paths.

I would now like to cross paths with a "Sugar Momma or Daddy" because I'm tired and would like to stop working.

...Just putting it out there.

… Just putting it out there.
Just a heads up …
I use the "F" word in the book.
For those of you a little squeamish about blasphemy,
I spoke to God and he told me to tell you,
it was okay.

Preface

I write this book on the eve of my retirement.

You have probably never heard of me. There may be a very slight possibility you recognize my name or maybe my face. But I have no delusions. Way before Kathy Griffin's *My Life On the D-List* I always teased, *"I've sky-rocketed to the middle."* (It birthed my script, *The Biggest Mistake of My Life.*)

When I was around eighteen, I sent my first comedy demo to a local, stereotypical, old, Jewish, cigar-chomping, talent booker named, Moe Shames. When I called, following up to see if he reviewed my tape, he replied, "Yeah, I saw it. And frankly, you have no talent."

He could have easily told me I wasn't ready yet, or I was too blue, or I wasn't the type of act he booked. But instead he decided to crush a young man's spirit ... if only for a day or two.

Years later whenever I was headlining on the east coast, Moe would regularly send his business card backstage and try to contact me.

It's a very small percentage of those who become famous. But I never really wanted that. I just wanted to do good work and hopefully follow the path to where I might eventually flourish and ultimately belong. Finding that place is also helpful if someone appreciates your work and opens a door or two for you.

I've worked in over forty countries, comedy-toured with some "names," done some television, a few movies, voiceovers, TV/film puppeteering, off-off-take-a-left-turn-off Broadway, producing, directing, writing, coaching, and I only did restaurant and temp work in my late teens.

But to this day I'm not sure I've discovered my true calling or complete expression. Although my ridiculously eclectic life experience through that search now serves me well when I get the very fulfilling opportunities to write, direct or show doctor a project.

Many say show business is ungrateful. But what business isn't? Stay for as long as it feeds you and *try* to make sure you have some money saved for when you can no longer wipe your own ass. And in my experience, try to make enough of a personal life and establish roots for yourself to stay "healthy." I rarely see that.

For years I've been told to write a book, but for whom? Who's gonna read, let alone buy another book about show business from someone you don't even know? My mother can't buy them all.

I could've gone on and on in this book about the development of the characters, or writing or the craft, but let's face it. Pages of pontification aren't what you're interested in.

I haven't gotten as far as some, and I've gotten farther than others who have tried to live a show business life. This is a little taste of my attempts to move up the ladder.

I never wanted to be the sad performer that sits around telling war stories of when he played "Waiter #2" in the third season of *Law and Order* and refers to show creator, Dick Wolf, as "Dick."

If he ever actually met or tried to converse with Mr. Wolf, I'm sure it went something like this.

GUY
Hi, Dick.
DICK
Hello ... Waiter #2.

(As a point of reference, I am the one person in New York City that has never been on an episode of *Law and Order*.)

This is the same kind of guy who will tell anyone who will listen, "*Oh — I'm on set today.*" Okay, ummm — no one asked. What forced pretention! I want to reply, "*Oh you're on set? I'm on couch.*" Go fuck yourself.

When writing this, it was extremely difficult not to blur the line between telling juicy stories that aren't always flattering to others *or* going negative, verbally (or the printed equivalent) bitch-slapping those who have wronged me.

I, like most, have been stolen from, bumped out, cheated, and screwed a multitude of times. That book would have been the size of the Old Testament.

This is just a bunch of weird, unrelated craziness tied together. And to be sure, these are nowhere near all of the stories.

I hope you like it. These are the highlights of my life ... so far.

The City Of Brotherly Love:
KYW-TV, *Dancin' On Air* & Miles Davis

When I was around fifteen years old, a neighbor who worked at WPHL-TV, Channel seventeen in Philadelphia gave me passes to dance on the TV show *Dancin' On Air*, a sort of *American Bandstand* rip off for the '80s trailer trash of the tri-state area.

I wasn't a dancer but that wasn't the point: I'd be on television. That, and I had passes to invite the prettiest girls in my class to score points since I had no "wooing" qualities.

One girl in particular who always had right of first refusal was Jennifer Genaro. OMG, I was in love with her from kindergarten through sixth grade. Then I was in love with Paul Scarfone from seventh to twelfth. Both had the qualities I fell for: Italian, smooth, olive skin. I'd sit behind Jennifer in class. The shampoo in her hair smelled so good. Petite, beautiful smile, big brown eyes … you get the picture.

The dance tickets were a waste on Jennifer because her mother would never let her date me. I was Jewish. I'm not sure how true of a reason that is, but Jen is now married and her mother is dead so, you know … my recollection is fact.

Meanwhile, my mother noticed that the TV show's producer, Mike Nise, a middle aged, disheveled, schlub of a guy would ogle her with overly demonstrative, octopus-like contact whenever she was in his presence. So like any good mother who wanted to help her son, she led him on until he gave me an internship.

Every day after school my mother would pick me up and drive thirty minutes to the station to work on *Dancin' on Air* and the national sister show *Dance Party USA* on the USA network. The only difference between the shows were the switched out hanging neon signs. That's about it, aside from the changing of clothes. NKOTB, Jack Wagner, a few of the Jacksons ... they all came through Wynnfield, PA. to WPHL-TV.

Years later after I'd moved on to bigger things, I stayed in touch with Mike Nise. He was very nice to me but as I grew up, I realized he was full of shit.

He'd say to me, "Michael hang on. I got *The Tonight Show* on the other line." I'm sure Mike was on with *The Tonight Show* ... for tickets. But he was a nice man who stepped in something good. I figured maybe he'd do it again.

As a sophomore in high school, I skipped morning class to be in the studio audience of a local morning talk show called *People Are Talking*, a franchise format being used in multiple markets.

It was hosted by people like *Extra's* Jerry Penacoli (I still have footage of my high school interview he was kind enough to give), *Comedy Tonight's* Bill Boggs, *The Wil Shriner Show's* Wil Shriner, and the *original* trash TV host, Richard Bey.

Richard was my favorite character. Sport coat, black tee shirt, jeans, cowboy boots, blue contacts, and make up so dark he could be either very tan or Pakistani. He'd wear the make up the rest of the day. Maybe it was for the attention, maybe a skin condition. I recall his very bulbous nose that bent to the right. He liked himself very much but hey, so did his viewing audience.

I was mesmerized by the set. A fake home made up of a living room and kitchen. So real! I couldn't keep my eyes off the big lumbering cameras, the prompters, especially the earpieces: listening to direction from some unknown person somewhere else.

It was then I heard the two words that hooked me: "STAND BY," and the red light went on. My heart pumped fast and hard. I didn't watch the show. I was too busy watching the floor manager. I was worried for her. Would she get Richard's attention to tell him to "wrap it up" or "go to break?" What if he was too engrossed? Her sign language was subtle and nonchalant. Fascinating.

When the audience was being led out to the lobby, I took a right and stepped into an elevator. I couldn't leave just yet. I was behind the big metal doors of KYW-TV3 where the magic happened for shows like *Evening Magazine*, *Check It Out*, *Eyewitness News*, and the late night horror show *Saturday Night Dead* starring Elvira rip off, "Stella" the man-eater from Manayunk. I was stopped once and asked if they could help me. I somehow pulled a name from the rolling credits I had just seen while seated in the studio audience, and without a blink, said I was waiting on Rob Daniels. Then I gave myself a tour of the station.

My father was chairperson of a telethon produced and broadcasted at the station. So that "gravitas" street cred and emboldening lineage, combined with my little infiltration, introduced me to on-air personality Nancy Glass, who later hosted and anchored several national programs. She was tall, blond haired, blue eyed and very funny on the air. A little crush had developed. (Me for her, of course... I mean, she didn't know me yet...) She introduced me to the director of programming, Lisa Nee. Local stations rarely have this position anymore since the mid '90s when budgets dried up for local shows with the exception of news, parades, and the black or Hispanic community outreach shows required by the broadcast regulators.

For some reason Lisa agreed to hire me as an intern. I was seventeen and the youngest intern ever hired at an NBC affiliate. She also offered to pay for my bus pass to and from the suburbs to the station in Center City, in addition to paying my parking on the one or two taping days I'd have to stay late. I don't know why or how this happened but up till then, it was the most exciting time of my life.

I had to convince my high school officials to allow me to be eligible for the work/study program, usually a curriculum for seniors going to Vo-Tech. They agreed, figuring I wasn't doing my homework anymore, so why make me go to the pointless electives? I would do the state required courses in the morning, and then go to work at the station: first KYW and later when my contract was up, I jumped to WCAU - CBS Radio, which I got after being the only applicant to drudge out into the worst blizzard of the decade for the interview.

KYW-TV had a groundbreaking history. It was the first nationally broadcasted station, home to *The Mike Douglas Show* and a springboard for many network personalities. It was also the last wave of what local television "was."

During my time at KYW, the network and Westinghouse Broadcasting would bring their test shows there before going national. So many stars came through. I remember Miles Davis coming to perform live on the morning talk show in front of a studio audience.

I was assisting the producers by moving everyone into place and keeping an eye on Mr. Davis as we got him in the makeup chair after a very late arrival. The makeup woman was Anne Amiko, a short, heavy, brunette who had worked on every star for the last twenty years who needed cosmetics, in addition to an opera singing cat, and the homeless guy on 5th and Market with alopecia.

Miles was leaning back in the chair like he was at the dentist. He had his pitch-black sunglasses on and was a little clammy looking. He wasn't moving a muscle. I figured he was either tired from the road or perhaps had a cold. (I was hoping for a heartbeat...) But eventually I heard the murmuring of the concerned associate producers. He had arrived high on — well, more than just life — which was not uncommon for him, especially in his final years.

As Anne was leaning over him applying makeup, Miles awoke from his embalmment, reached around the big woman's body, cupped her ample behind with two hands and attempted to pull her up onto the chair. With a *"Come here baby!"* Miles laughed, Anne shrieked, she got a slap on her ass, he got a slap on his face and the moment ended as fast as it began. But he was now conscious and semi-alert, so all were happy.

I escorted him to the studio and handed him off to the floor manager during the commercial break. The band was set, Miles took his mark. There was a countdown, the red light, and host Bill Boggs introduced the legend, Miles Davis.

The band started playing and Miles stood there holding his horn, bobbing his head to the music. A minute in and he still hadn't played a note. Then, finally, the band led him into his solo, he pulled the famous horn to his lips and he gave one blow ... and that was it. One note. The rest of the song he swayed. Not to the music, but the precursor of perhaps falling over. It's possible he didn't even know he was in the middle of a broadcast. And if he did, maybe he thought he was still playing.

The producers were nuts over the expense and the embarrassment. They ended up shooting around him. Bill tried to get a short interview out of him, the audience applauded, then we went to break and his people quickly hustled (well, carried) him out the door to the limo.

To me, this was great television. I have seen and been on both sides of many moments like this over the years where you just have to shrug your shoulders and say, "Fuck it, it's show business."

I Should've Stolen The Grammy

KYW-TV3 - Philadelphia was a training ground for top talk show producers working today. I worked for Ed Glavin (*The Ellen DeGeneres Show*), Glenn Davish (*The View*), Lynn MacCauley (*Ricki Lake*) and others.

I was originally assigned to a Saturday morning teen show called, *Check It Out*, with executive producer, Janet King Johnson. She was a slim, African American woman with a flat topped afro, probably in her thirties and she scared the piss out of me.

Janet had no qualms in exhibiting her displeasure of my presence. She told me numerous times in the first week that I was a seventeen-year-old high school kid with no education in television when there were countless college students majoring in the field. "You being assigned to me makes my job harder, not easier," she'd say.

She was right. I didn't know terms or technology. She would turn to me and rattle off ten things to be done. I'd say okay, get out of her sight, then ask someone, *anyone* to decipher her list. It was usually an engineer that helped after taking pity on me.

One time she asked for time coded, blacked out, blank tapes for the next taping. It turned out the tapes given to me were not time coded so, when she went to edit, she couldn't find anything without viewing the entire tape of raw footage back and forth. I'm sure it gave her an extra three hours of work. She loathed me.

Another time I was carrying a pile of videotapes past the bulk tape eraser machine. It was the size of a huge office copier. Instead of taping over shows repeatedly, you put the videotapes on the machine, flipped the switch and the magnetizing erased the tapes, clean. The machine was on as I walked by and ruined my tapes.

I got into the groove eventually. It was mostly grunt work. Month three I asked Janet if my name would ever be on the credits. She said if and when she felt I earned it but to not hold my breath. A month later after I brought back dinner for a late night taping for everyone, she called me into the editing room and showed me my name scrolling by. We hugged. After that I was an equal ... an equal who still did the grunt work.

I had my own desk and handled many of the shows' responsibilities. When things were slow, I would sneak off to other shows to help (a.k.a. get in the way) and mostly to learn.

One of the tough things was realizing that, while I loved the technical side of production, the performance side was something I also wanted very much. I watched the hosts of all these shows and knew that kind of personality was inside me. But my quiet, shy nature was still holding me back. I was also self-conscious of a nasal voice and a lazy "S" in my speech.

Then one day I was opening the mail at my desk when I read a notice from the Grammy Awards press department informing us that if our station wanted press passes to cover the show, we should contact them by mail with our producer, camera man, and host names.

Janet had no interest in covering the show — but I did. I wanted to be a host or reporter and I needed to show someone I could do it. So I filled out the paperwork using my home address to receive the passes (clearly pre-911).

I knew nothing about music, but I knew someone who did. I knew Mark Doctrow from a youth group I was in. He was older than me and, more importantly, he was MTV crazy. Madonna was his specialty. He knew and followed everything. He was from Harrisburg and it was clear his obsession was based on the necessity of getting out of his small town life once he was old enough.

I called him up and told him he'd be my producer and feed me relevant questions as the stars came by. He readily agreed and even got his father's tuxedo shop to supply our wares. The cameraman was an a/v teacher at another friend's high school.

In retrospect it probably looked out of place having a home video camera next to professional television cams on the red carpet, but I dressed the camera in NBC peacock logos from the KYW art department and got a news logo cube to go around my microphone. We were all set.

Then the passes came in the mail. I couldn't believe it! We got our train tickets, went up together, walked over to Radio City, checked in and stepped behind the barricades onto the press pit. Most of the stars went in through the back door but we saw Billy Joel, Cyndi Lauper, Herbie Hancock, Jody Watley, and I interviewed Howard Stern, who was so incredibly nice to me. He even pushed other reporters aside and moved me to the front of the velvet ropes. This was also going to be Michael Jackson's first television appearance in four years, performing "Man in the Mirror."

They then moved everyone inside to the pressroom. It was the first time the Grammy Awards had returned to New York in several years and now I could see why. Radio City Music Hall was a death trap. The pressrooms were in the upper levels of the building and the press was squeezed into very old, very small, very warm, creaky elevators. Total fire hazard. I honestly don't know how the fire marshal allowed it. Maybe the Grammy producers made Liza Minnelli distract him with a long story about how she and her mother both married gay guys.

Upon exiting the lift, we were given official programs, formats, and network/satellite feed packets. Individual cameras weren't allowed due to space, so all news outlets patched their recorders into one pool camera system provided by the Grammys. Mike, our cam guy, sat in the back while Mark and I sat only three or four rows back from the "step and repeat" platform and microphone.

I sat next to Rob Garrett from ABC News, across from Mary Hart of *Entertainment Tonight*, and behind Rona Barrett, famed entertainment broadcaster and columnist who was probably in her late sixties, more glammed up than some stars, and who became the thorn in every journalist's side that evening.

You see, once the presenters and winners exit the stage, they go upstairs to each pressroom (print, TV or radio). The press only gets three to five questions with the talent before they are rushed off. So asking a bad question fucks the chances of everyone else in the room for getting picked by the moderator to ask their question. I didn't realize this until an hour in.

Ms. Barrett's first question was to a Grammy winner: "You didn't win last year, but you won this year. How does that make you feel?" Okay, the room accepted that without a blink.

Her next time chosen she asked a presenter: "You get to see these people win. How does that make you feel?" There was a grumbling and fidgeting around me. I got an eye roll from Rob Garrett.

Her next opportunity was quizzing a winning producer: "How does this make you feel tonight?" Now I, a seventeen-year-old high school student had joined the angry mob in asking the moderator to stop picking Rona Barrett. Somehow I was now one of the boys. No one seemed to care or notice that I was a fetus.

Eventually I needed to go stretch my legs. I got up and walked to the back of the room and into a dark hallway. I looked down and couldn't believe what I saw ... a box full of Grammys. Apparently back then, the awards were dummy awards and not inscribed until later. After the stars came through the pressrooms they dumped them into this cardboard box! I was alone for a good minute. I was in a panic. Do I steal a Grammy? Walking by a random, unsecured pile of *anything*, I'd question taking one. And these were Grammys. There's a pile of Grammys right there. Finally my ethical dilemma/life of crime was interrupted by pedestrian traffic.

I returned to the room right before they brought a few of us down, group by group, to sit in the theater for a segment or two. I interviewed Liza Minnelli, Patrick Swayze, and a handful of others. It was a good night.

Mark Doctrow later moved to New York, got a job at MTV and became Madonna's exclusively requested producer. He now works for CNN.

Janet King Johnson was rumored to have subsequently worked on *The Oprah Winfrey Show*. I've thought about finding her, but why poke a sleeping lion?

First Night In New York Comedy
& Rodney Dangerfield

Seeing someone in his or her element is an aphrodisiac, I discovered very early on. Like anyone seen doing what they do best, the super attractive people who might not normally take notice or consider me, would watch me perform and then throw room keys, underwear, and themselves at me, figuratively speaking ... except for when I opened for Tom Jones. (At the end of his shows, the stage looked like my mother's hamper.) I had this awesome, superhero power. As I matured I tried to use "my powers" for good and not evil! I'm speaking about once the act was polished. It took a few years to get there.

It was my third or fourth time doing comedy in Philly when local headliner, Big Daddy Graham, told me about a club in New York that was making room for new showcase spots. A showcase was three to five minutes of stage time given to a new comic to try stuff out in between the three professional acts. Nowadays there's no such thing because the public is paying for a comedy show and getting twelve guys doing six minutes each, most of them sucking.

For the record, the meat grinder format is disrespectful to the audience, the comic, but most importantly, to the craft. Six minutes is not enough time to create a beginning, middle and end of anything an audience could be truly invested in, especially if a comic's piece is different than the last seven guys. It's whiplash and the audience can't switch gears fast enough. But I digress.

I drive up to New York on a Saturday night in my Nissan

Sentra (a.k.a. the juice can on wheels) to the address I was given, 78th & Broadway, home to Stand Up New York.

The club was dark and there were lots of people pacing by the bar … all comics. I couldn't find Big Daddy, but I put my name on the list to get stage time. While I was waiting, I watched a short, tomboy type of girl on stage … really calm and understated. After my set we talked for a bit and a year later, I saw her on *Saturday Night Live*. Almost eighteen years later, Janeane Garofalo and I acted together in *The Ten*.

But after Stand Up New York, I hung around tryin' to figure out what people were doing next. One of the New Jersey comics invited me to jump in his car to go do a late night set on the east side at Dangerfield's, then still owned by Rodney. I was told he never came to the club.

Some of the comics hanging out were performing and some were there just to shoot the shit: Bob Saget, Richard Jeni, Richard Belzer, Dennis Wolfberg, and a crowd of others. Clearly they had all been doing this a while. I could feel the grit in their souls.

The show began and I was the third to go up when Rodney Dangerfield, his wife, and another couple entered the club and sat down. The manager came up to me and said, "Rodney is gonna do a few minutes, then you." I was sure this wasn't happening. Somewhere between blacking out and shitting my pants, I decided I must have heard him wrong.

The man who never comes to his own club was called to the stage. The place went nuts and I was ready to puke. I turned to the bar with flop sweat. I was tryin' to act cool as all the comics were hooting and teasing me because no one wants to follow animals, children, or Rodney Dangerfield (or the animal child, Rodney Dangerfield…).

Richard Jeni put a hand on my shoulder and gave me this advice: "When ya get up there, don't try to be slick. Listen to what you're feeling and just say it. Be honest and give it up to the audience. They'll love you for it. And if they don't love you for it, they'll at least pity ya."

Rodney did ten minutes, killed, then sat down. I was introduced as a new comic and received a nice, polite applause. Notes in hand, I walked up on stage, lights in my face, hands shaking, holding onto the mic stand for dear life.

The comics were laughing and enjoying the spectacular crash-n-burn of another comic until I heard Jeni yell to me, "Tell the truth!" when I cleared my throat and said, "It's my third night in comedy and I have to go on after Rodney-Fucking-Dangerfield." Everyone laughed and clapped at my predicament. I then proceeded to do a few Rodney riffs. I tugged on my invisible tie and collar, "Hey, hey! My wife is a terrible cook. How can toast have bones in it?" I was impersonating and mocking Rodney right in front of him. Everyone laughed, then he shouted, "Okay, ya little bastard! Do your own stuff!"

I don't really remember the rest. I did four more minutes off my notes, got some applause, then went to the bar and got drunk.

Years later I wrote a script as a vehicle for Richard Jeni just months before he killed himself. Terrible.

I had gone to the clubs in Philly a few times on open mic night and even then I thought it was a shitty deal. Your audience was made up of a bunch of wanna-be comics. As you'd perform they'd either be working on their own stuff or stealing yours. Either way, you were never going to get an accurate assessment of your work because they weren't a paying audience.

Meanwhile, my family was falling on hard times and I thought this would be my most immediate way out of the darkness. Who had the time or money for four (or twelve) years of college? Not me.

I already knew how to promote. So I gave some thought as to the style and persona I wanted to create as a comic stage personality and created press releases and a bio around it. I finally got a five minute slot at Philly's The Comedy Works on 2nd and Chestnut. The club was a major stop for the big touring comics. The problem was, I didn't really have an act yet.

But I *did* have a list I had been compiling of every booker and stage producer in the country. And now, I was going to finally have a tape of my set on a legitimate stage to send to them.

It was a good set ... for a beginner, or a child ... or someone who was selected by the Make a Wish Foundation, but definitely not good enough to show professionals. Who the hell knows that at the time though, right? It was mostly dick jokes with a puppet that barely moved, almost like it had a stroke and the voice sounded like ... uhhh, my own. Sending out those demos probably kept me from working for another two years!

This was also the beginning of a very bad habit, the need for security and getting ahead in life causing me to panic and rush things before putting in the full time to my craft. The cake is not finished and in turn, cannot sustain. It took nearly fifteen years to figure that out.

The Winona Ryder Experience

Again, with all of my stories, there will be no mud-flinging ... at least publicly. It's unbecoming and although I know you are begging for a train wreck story here, I love Winona Ryder as a person.

David Wain, the co-creator of the improv group *The State* (formerly *Stella*) as seen on MTV and later CBS, had produced his first film. It was a college cult classic titled, *Wet, Hot, American Summer* with a cast of unknowns that are A-List celebrities today.

A few years later, Winona Ryder was plastered across every medium for shoplifting. A year after that, she decided to make a quiet come back doing small roles in small but unique films. One being David's next film, *The Ten*, referring to ten comedy vignettes based on the Ten Commandments. Winona's commandment? "Thou Shall Not Steal," of course.

I remember going in for a costume fitting a few weeks prior to shooting. Winona and I were scheduled the same time. I was told she was in the wardrobe dressing area and she wanted to meet me. She was extremely cute and petite. No entourage, just chatting it up with the dresser. Girl talk.

Like most show people, she wasn't inhibited to change clothes wherever it was required or available. She came over to meet me half dressed and we shook hands while alterations were being made to her clothing. She finished dressing and we chatted about where we lived, what job we had just arrived from, and the usual getting to know you, small talk before I made my exit. Once shooting began, I experienced a taste of the amazing Winona Ryder phenomena.

First and foremost, the paparazzi were everywhere. When

we were outside, it was extremely disruptive. Legally, they had to remain behind an invisible line just behind production. Bobbing up and down, back and forth around the crew and equipment, snapping away at her every move.

I felt bad. Many of us felt almost protective of her... I know I did. In fact, between takes, I'd casually stand to her left or right side, directly in the line of their shot. The paparazzi would yell, threatening to make it harder for us to work if we kept "pulling that kind of nonsense."

Winona had an amazing ability to break character, ask a question of the director, then "turn it back on," returning immediately to the scene. On/off, on/off. I can't say the crying or scenes requiring hysterics were deep, gut wrenching, or rich per se, but 1) that wasn't this genre; 2) she was still full out; and 3) what the fuck did I know? It was clear she knew film acting; angles, performance levels, matching emotionally what was needed for the camera and what wasn't.

In between takes she'd step outside and smoke alone. By day two I'd go hang with her and bum one.

We had just finished a scene with a surreal rehearsal involving her, David Wain, and me standing around a bed actually discussing the best way for her to, and I quote, "fuck a dummy."

Winona had to simulate sex with a puppet. "I'll do whatever you want but I don't wanna be 'the man'." Of course she was referring to her physical positioning and remaining visually in the feminine role. I thought that was a fascinating insight for protecting herself and her brand.

She and I chatted one on one quite a bit over the next week or so. Unsolicited, she was very forthcoming about boyfriends, about acting, about her family. I thought it was fascinating that she never owned a computer. She just didn't want to be subjected to anything written about her.

By the last days of shooting, she'd hang on me like a bud. We'd hug goodnight. The last day together she took me aside and congratulated me on my first film, telling me I was a very good actor. She was probably just being nice, but it was something she didn't have to say.

I only recall one afternoon of diva-like inklings. I think she just needed to remind herself or the producers of who needed to be treated special. Again, this book isn't a public mudslinger. You'll have to call me to hear what took place.

At one point she and I took a walk through the neighborhood. Even in a supermarket, the flip phones were up all around her. Awful. It's no wonder some celebs can get socially awkward. As we walked down the street, the paparazzi were literally five feet in front of us walking backwards. I'd joke, "Come on guys, can't I get a moment's peace?" One of the men asked for her autograph. Knowing these guys sell the signatures on Ebay, she apologized and explained that she only signs for children. One of them cursed her out right to her face!

Half a year later the film went to Sundance. The night of the first viewing and Q&A session, she walked into the green room, saw me, ran over and gave me a huge hug. We exchanged pleasantries and she told me her father loved my comedy DVD that I gave her so much that he watched it once a week.

A highlight was when she, my brother, and I were at a cocktail hour. She grabbed my arm and said, "Come here. I want to introduce you to my friend Tony." I turned around. It's Anthony Hopkins. What the hell am I gonna say to Anthony Hopkins? (No — nothing about fava beans. I know you were thinking it.) We ended up chatting about his directorial debut at the festival. He was extremely charming and engaging.

Later that month I was going to play a club in the west village near her New York apartment. I asked her if she wanted to go. She replied, "Really? I've never been to a comedy club before!" Someone in their 30s has never been to a comedy club? Some lead — well, just a different life. I have met so many star actors that play roles of common people doing common things that they themselves have never experienced due to their celebrity bubble.

Winona and I did not stay in touch. I discovered that for most actors, you bond during a project, and then that's it. You are rarely if ever pen pals. You just add it to your book and move on to the next experience.

Now what happened to my wallet?

Don Rickles:
If You Like Me, Insult Me

Joan Rivers was split-billing with Don Rickles. We hugged backstage. I remember I wanted a photo of us. She had just gotten an acid face peel and her face had strawberry splotches so she agreed to the photo but made her assistant take it from way down the hall! She then said, "You wanna meet Don?" She grabbed my arm and we walked down the hall and into dressing room number two.

I had been on a stage with Rickles once before when I competed in the finals of the Jay Leno — *Tonight Show* Comedy Competition around 1992. But I was a fan years before with a signed autograph of him hanging on my wall at age thirteen or fourteen. Later, I kept my pot stash in the back of that box frame. My sister would ask where my "eighth" was and I'd reply, "It's behind Don Rickles."

Joan and I walked into his dressing room. One of the last of the Sinatra cohorts, Don was sitting on a chair next to a simple fruit platter watching the football game. In true Rat Pack form, he wore black tux pants, shoes, white shirt, and a red crushed velvet robe with his initials on the pocket.

Joan introduced us and reminded Don of our prior meeting. "Oh yeah, the puppet was funny. You? Not so much." He grinned and offered me a seat.

Joan wanted to check with Don on the makeup she applied covering her acid peel marks. "Don, how do I look?"

The banter began with Rickles's reply: "Aren't you gonna put on any makeup?"

JOAN: "I did put on makeup!"

DON: "Jesus. Looks like you were dragged down the street by a bus!"

Watching two comedy legends go at it is indescribable. It's like watching Ali and Foreman, only with more laughter and slightly more blood. I know they're legends but they're bickering legends in that loving show biz way.

I am rarely star struck. But I couldn't help myself. I had to share with this man what he meant to me.

"Mr. Rickles," I said, "You are the reason I got into comedy."

He fired back, "Well that was a mistake." Then, to nobody: "What's on channel two?"

Some comic's method is to work and tinker with the same act material for twenty years like Leno or Seinfeld, believing you're never done chiseling away. While others throw it out and create all new stuff every year like Louie CK or Ricky Gervias. These are two equally viable philosophies. Don's show was flawless. His act was down to a science. And smartly, he never did any stage act material on television, ever. That way it was new for the live audiences.

Thanks to Joan and Don's wife Barbara, I got to open for Don more than a few times. During that time he taught me two things that were immeasurable to my mental and comedic health:

1) You are *not* a limited performer if you can't cater to multiple audiences. Find *your* audience.

2) When doing stand-up, if you are going to open the door to working the audience, you'd better know how to do it and do it without bashing people cheaply. Don taught me how to listen, think, filter, and then deliver all simultaneously! (Shout-Out: I was also able to fine-tune this skill by watching Las Vegas staple, Cork Proctor, who literally had no act, just his educated wit.)

The Day Ben Affleck
Almost Kicked My Ass

For a few years I made some money being hired as a fake guest speaker for entertainment at corporate events. For example, during the after dinner awards and speeches I might be introduced as the CEO's brother. I'd then go up and "roast" my bro' as the "favorite child" and get laughs, as I'd "out" all of his supposed family secrets.

Another time I was hired to play the guest speaker at a corporate weekend for architects. My speech entailed my design for a mental hospital under the ocean, explaining that being underwater relieved the pressure on the brain for the patients, which in turn, allowed for medical procedures to be accomplished more successfully.

This type of performance has to be done meticulously. It's a very slow burn. If rushed, the audience will know they're being bamboozled and the arc of the piece will be cut too short for the comedy. The longer you can go without being questioned on the absurdity of what you're selling, the better it is. More importantly, you're being paid. So to finish in five minutes, would be bad. (That would've been fine for me in a few situations...)

As I continued to explain the partnership between myself and the medical community, it was clear I was focusing on the mental issues more than the structural details of my architectural accomplishment (invention, innovation). Of course the crowd began murmuring and hands raised to question me.

I explained it was like working with paper mache. "You

blow up a big balloon, cover it in cement, then pop the balloon in the middle!" The more I went on, the more agitated and verbal the crowd got.

"That's absurd!" someone yelled. The more I talked about the mental stability of the patients, the crazier I became.

Yelling and throwing things, I was finally dragged off stage. The CEO then came on and revealed the hoax. I returned for my bow.

It was this event that brought me to Ben Affleck.

I received a call from the PR department that was handling the Affleck/Lopez movie, *Gigli*. I was to be planted into the press core for the all-day junket to make a disruptive, combative scene. Not enough to be arrested, just enough to get thrown out and create some press. They would not confirm whether Ben was in on it and there would be no one to help me if it turned ugly. It was $500, a press pass, and an "oh yeah... you'll be on your own..."

I arrived at the New York hotel early in the morning where the junket was taking place and picked up my credentials. I was listed as being with the publication, the *Las Vegas Sun*. Ben wouldn't be there till much later in the day. I had to attend from the beginning so I could integrate with the press and so I wouldn't/didn't expose myself as a plant. I should've asked for more money. It was exhausting to banter while being nervous all day!

Ben and J-Lo had just broken up so before his arrival we were all instructed not to ask about her. Of course once he entered and started taking questions, I stood up and asked a point blank Jennifer Lopez question. There was annoyance from Ben. The other press people were amused. The moderator corrected my lack of protocol.

In the middle of him chatting away, I took out a disposable camera, walked right up to his face, snapped a photo and walked back to my seat while winding the film to the next frame. People thought I was nuts.

About eight minutes in, my third question wasn't being answered. I wasn't even being called on. It was time to bump it up. I yelled, "You don't seem very pleased to be here Ben. I mean, you're not Matt Damon! When's that second Oscar winning script coming out?"

We got into a yelling match! I stormed right up to the dais pointing and flapping my arms! I have no idea if he was in on it or not, but he seemed livid.

The studio people were having a fit and the press cameras were flashing away — just as planned. I was escorted out while still snapping photos and thumbing the loud "advance" button on my Kodak disposable.

There was some exposure on *Extra* or one of those shows and a few newspapers about a rogue reporter making a scuffle. No one knew the real story except me. And now, *us* ...

I stopped doing those kinds of things because it's super stressful and frankly, my insurance wasn't good enough for the risk of getting my ass kicked.

Years later I used this kind of "reality" marketing strategy when I was brainstorming with the PR team for Jay Johnson's Broadway show, *My Two and Only*. Some of you may recall Jay when he co-starred in the TV show *Soap* as "Chuck Campbell" along with his ventriloquist sidekick, "Bob."

I wanted to contact the local press just before the six o'clock news, informing them that there was a suicide jumper on top of the Helen Hayes Theatre. They would arrive to find "Bob" screaming and threatening to "do it"!

The Road:
Seinfeld, Romano, Wolfberg, Foxworthy & A Little Regret

When I was in fifth grade, David Culp and I did "Who's On First" for the talent show and became instant celebrities. (I closed the show by singing a camp favorite, "God Bless My Underwear.") The first graders were in awe of us. Over the last twenty years since then ...

I had to have a manager follow me to my car so a bunch of hicks didn't come beat me up after a show. (In all fairness I was nineteen and brand new at comedy, playing a diner in the sticks on a Wednesday night, so I was kind of askin' for it.)

I've had a drink thrown at me, followed by the glass.

I've played a house where the crowd in the balcony was deaf and the main floor group was all Russian, so they either couldn't hear me up top or couldn't understand me down below.

I've been dragged to the floor and put in a headlock by the same drunk twice in the same show.

I've been snowed in at a club with an angry audience (neither of which were my doing).

I accidentally brought a deaf mute on stage who wouldn't stop a guttural moaning sound that turned the audience, crew, and myself white and sweaty.

I once inquired who was having a birthday at a front table resulting in being out-yelled by thirty Down syndrome audience members seated in the back responding, "I'm having a birthday!" over and over and over and over until I had to leave the stage. Upon my return, I stepped into the audience only to be surrounded by them, continuing the birthday chant and heavily petting me to the floor. (People with Down syndrome have super strength in case you didn't know.)

I've gone on stage bleeding, broken, and puking in between sets. But hey, quit show business? It must go on.

The Road was the hard knocks of the trenches. But I hit a crossroads when introduced to the casino circuit. The whole Vegas thing was, and is, a weird microcosm of entertainment.

Nice hotel rooms, my name was on marquees, my face was on billboards as "comedy guest star." I was offered good money and was in one place for an extended time where critics could come review me. I felt like I was really doing well. I had a career now and I could finally stop running, or just surviving, and smell the roses a little.

In those Las Vegas shows, I was put in between the showgirls and singers. I would walk down the staircase at the end of the show and the audience would rise to standing ovations. As an opening act for celebrities in casinos, I would finish my set in front of 500 or 5000 people to roaring applause before the star act came on. I got hooked.

I would continue to occasionally play the comedy clubs to keep my teeth sharp and stay connected. I did not realize I had bypassed something that would affect my career twenty years later.

Years ago, comedienne Elayne Boosler got her own room in Vegas and she was shunned as a sellout, no longer legit to the other comics. Who knew she was ahead of her time? Now everyone wants that gig.

But I should've stayed in the trenches of the club scene. I think my career would have been in a much different place.

There's nothing wrong with my career per se. I haven't had a "normal" job since I was nineteen. But being on my own that young, I went for the immediate money and glitz instead of the grit. There's equal hardship to each road but the club scene can provide you with a base for more industry legitimacy. Who knew?

I still go back to the clubs. I know how to do them and I do them well. I also do it to remind myself of the most basic, organic, comedy expression. When you open for a star, do TV, a revue show, or even (dare I say it?), a cruise ship, you take what you learned from the raw, exposed, freeing experience of a club, then polish and edit it for the higher-end clientele and venues.

If I had stayed in the trenches, I'd like to believe I'd be playing the types of venues and would have received the kind of exposure where I could have grown more, had a bigger following and been treated a little better.

If Twitter was around when I was at my peak, my followers might have been in the thousands! Today, I'm around 320. Twitter + Self Worth = Therapy. (This is the *real* "new Math...") I'm not tortured about it anymore, but I was when I cared so much more about the ego of "climbing the ladder."

Many east and west coast comics always had a disdain for variety or "prop" acts. Jay Leno has always said he felt the performer was using the prop instead of writing good material. I think that's ridiculous. While there are plenty of hacky, cheesy prop acts, there are just as many hacky stand-up comics. And for someone like myself, who eventually *added* ventriloquism, well, I think my job has aspects that are twice as hard, trying to achieve honest, strong material. Because now it's for "two individuals" along with the technical side, making the set ups, punch lines, and segues conversational as well as using, or ignoring, the reality of there being a puppet. To this day I still have clubs tell me, "We don't hire ventriloquists, only legit comics."

I loved stand-up. But once the comedy boom hit in the late '80s and everyone had ten minutes of material (even my cousin's Rabbi booked *The Tonight Show*). The ventriloquism made me more sellable and bookable, not just another guy talking in front of a mic. I do miss the days as a stand-up comic just walking myself into the club. Dragging around props can blow.

I came into comedy at the birth and boom of the big comedy era when there was a real paying club circuit. In that circuit, my favorite acts were not the household name comics. I loved the road guys ... the comic's comics.

Basile: Looked like a bearded Andrew Dice Clay, bad ass. He'd walk on to some hard rock music in his leather and shades. He'd swallow lighter fluid and blow fire. At the end of the music he'd sharply remove his sunglasses to reveal crazy, crossed eyes and a gay voice, shocking the audience into laughter.

Clause Meyers: A German comedian who would do thirty-five minutes of killer material about being in America, Hitler, and the like. Suddenly he'd drop the accent and admit he was "just fucking with ya" and his real name was Chris something. Then do fifteen more minutes of killer material as an American with a few German callbacks. Ugh — it was amazing every time I saw it. I still remember his opening joke. It went something like, "Ze vorld believes that ze Germans are obsessed with numeric organization. Zis is completely false (ahem) ... Joke number von!"

As I traveled, I especially loved the comedy variety acts like The Legendary Wid, a guy who had two moving boxes full of crap. He only spoke his sentences through the props in the boxes. If he couldn't find the right prop to make out the word he needed, then everyone was screwed. I don't know if it was his plan, but it was Genius. He had to headline... The only way you could follow him was with a bulldozer.

The Great Tomsoni & Company, aka The Wizard of Warsaw, aka The World's Foremost Polish Magician with his old, gum-cracking, shlepper of an assistant with a big rack. Her name was Igor: "His humps are on the wrong side." To their friends they're known as John and Pam Thompson and have been the parents of modern day magic. When PETA was having a "bird" regarding the dove harnesses magicians used to hide the animals in their jackets, John constructed a new design. They have played every major stage around the world and every TV variety show there was. They were in every magic book and have been asked to consult for Criss Angel, David Copperfield, Penn and Teller, and everyone else. When I was seventeen, Igor (Pam) went to the mall with me and pretended to be my mother, signing the permission slip for me to get an earring. (Left ear thank you very much.)

By 1990-91, I was coming into the scene as an opener or middle act on the bill alongside people who had already been doin' comedy for five to ten years including Seinfeld, Romano,

Foxworthy, Wolfburg, Garofalo ... The clubs were exciting and so much better than comedy performed on TV. Many think TV ruined stand-up comedy, not only for the acts, but for the audiences. They just don't realize it.

I do believe that home viewing audiences got used to edited, six minute snippets of humor in front of audiences that were prepped or warmed up. It made people think that's how it should come off in person at a club all the time.

Whose Line Is It Anyway? shoots for hours! Then they edit together the best parts. When you go to watch live improv, it can take a while to chisel out the nuggets of comedy. Then the audience leaves thinking the performers weren't that good.

I remember working at a club with Lewis Black before he became famous. He was *amazing*. That shaking and yelling he does on TV is nothing compared to when you see him on stage with time for a buildup. He would start talking about something and would slowly get agitated. He couldn't get the words out. His face would turn red. His hands would start shaking like he wanted a neck to choke. Then he would climax by grabbing the mic stand and banging it on the floor five or six times like a psycho at his breaking point. The audience would hold their breath watching the highs and lows of a man who was ready to have a heart attack at any second!

Unfortunately television doesn't allow for that kind of time to build the character arc. So nowadays he just goes right to the shaking and mock-anger. It's a shame you are missing out on the layers. It was artful.

These stories are probably only interesting to me, but screw you. Get your own book.

THE CONDO CIRCUIT
a.k.a. GOD'S WAITING ROOM

The Florida condo circuit seems to be a venue that you do either at the beginning of your career or at the end.

There are a series of retirement villages home to thousands of senior citizens. The communities are complete with convenience stores, golf courses and their very own theater. An entertainment coordinator books everything from karaoke night to the headlining roster of the auditorium. He is also the host (a.k.a. camp director).

I was around twenty-two with a very new act of perhaps twenty, semi-solid minutes of material, when I got a call to do a week of villages from Miami down to Marina Del Ray.

First stop — Century Village, home to a 2500 seat auditorium. The backstage walls were covered in 8x10 photos of the biggest names down to the unknowns and performers who were still working like dogs, beating the dead horse that once was their talent, before extinction. There was money to be made here, but I found out, it was at a cost.

Unlike having an evening, going out to dinner, then paying for a ticket to a show, the entertainment was brought to the village and plunked down almost nightly at the villagers' feet. There was no real investment to enjoy themselves. They were the judge and jury, waiting to be entertained, or at least sucked up to. They, the old people, ran this show.

At 6:00 p.m. the walkers, wheelchairs, scooters and a centipede of golf carts would exit their cottages and, like Moses through the desert, or zombies after midnight, make their way up the hill to the auditorium for another serving of fresh meat.

About forty minutes before show time, I was approached by the entertainment director:

ENTERTAINMENT DIRECTOR
No innuendo in the act.
ME
Oh — okay.
ENTERTAINMENT DIRECTOR
And you cannot go into the audience. People in the balcony won't be able to see and they'll want their two dollars back.
ME
Oh.
ENTERTAINMENT DIRECTOR
And no audience participation. The last thing we need is someone breaking a hip.

Motherfucker — that's my whole act! What am I gonna do for thirty minutes?

Tonight I was opening for Don Cornell: a former member (I assume they meant formerly alive) of the singing group, The Four Lads. Don was a low-res, photocopy of Sinatra: tux, salt-n-pepper hair, a cigarette, and an attitude.

His wife and manager pulled the director/host away for some notes, then it was showtime.

The host went out and, after making some announcements, went down the roster of "talent" they had in store in the coming weeks. The audience would "ooh" and "aah" at the return of unknowns only appreciated by this weird bubble of entertainment.

ENTERTAINMENT DIRECTOR
And Tuesday night, former child star, Bobby Breen, will return!
AUDIENCE
OOOOOOH!
ENTERTAINMENT DIRECTOR
The Mickey Finn Show!
AUDIENCE
OOOOOH!

These people would respond to anything recognizable. I wanted to shout out:

"George Washington will be here!" — *"OOOOHH!"*

"... and a phonograph player!" — *"AAAHHH"*

Somehow, I squeezed out a full thirty minutes. I bowed, grabbed my prop trunk (there was no stage crew) and I exited the front wing, only to find the host and Don Cornell's wife having a cow.

HOST
You were way over time! Don is very upset!
WIFE
Thirty-two minutes? It's throwing everything off!

As far as I was concerned, this Don Cornell person could go fuck himself. I'd just pulled a rabbit out of my ass on that stage. What's two extra minutes, and why was everyone kissing this nobody's ass?

Don walks by, flicks his ash at me and says, "Hey kid — less, is more." and continues onto the stage.

When I finished the second show, I bowed, grabbed my prop trunk and exited once again into the front wing, "clocking" Don with my trunk and knocking him to the ground. It was dark and he was in the wrong wing. Needless to say, we didn't say goodbye.

I threw my stuff in the car and went to do the later show at another village. This time, opening for singer, Jack Jones (voice of "The Love Boat").

I remember Jack was in the middle of a ballad and he wandered to one side of the stage.

The audience on the other side of the room started screaming in old, witch-like voices, "We can't hear youuuuuuu!" "Some of us sit on this side!" Just awful. My only solace was knowing I'd be done soon and they'd be dead soon.

After the show, I was making my way through the lobby, and was stopped over and over by people telling me how good I was. I was shocked. They gave me nothing for thirty minutes! Apparently I wasn't doing poorly. These people just don't feel the need to respond. I was in *their* house.

These are also the places where celebs drop off their elderly parents. I was approached by Woody Allen's mother as well as Fran Drescher's, who assumed I knew "Frannie." Of course, it is very possible these people weren't related at all. They were pretty senior.

The Queen Of England Is Chatty.
Will & Kate Are Nice

It was 1993. I was playing in a long running show at a hotel in one of the Caribbean islands still governed by England when it was announced that Her Royal Majesty, Queen Elizabeth II and Prince Phillip, the Duke of Edinburgh, would be making a tour of the British Commonwealth. Due to her age, it would probably be her last visit.

I also heard through one of the establishment's VPs that the hotel I was performing at was beginning a major renovation since they were chosen to host a twelve o'clock tea ceremony upon Her Majesty's arrival. It was then I decided I had to be at the ceremony, and more importantly, *in* the receiving line.

This was not the first time I made my way into things I wasn't invited to. (See: The Grammy Award, William-Morris Agency, or KYW-TV). The first step was easy. The cast was already invited to view the ceremony, but from behind the velvet ropes. (Velvet ropes do not a prison make...)

When the day finally came, the cast went over together. Dresses, suits, ties. I however, was hiding a few other items: My hotel ID badge, a pair of sunglasses, and my usual cunning.

We got to the hotel and made our way to the lush hotel patio and garden. I made a pit stop to the back office of the check-in desk where I procured a clipboard and some fake paperwork that I shoved into the clip, then rejoined the group.

I surveyed the area. The general public, dignitaries, the press, and three security teams were present: the hotel security, the Royal Bahamian police, and Her Majesty's team.

This was my moment. I slid on my glasses; clipped on my

badge as if it were something "official" for the event, pulled out the clipboard and stepped over the velvet ropes.

I kept a low profile but pretended to survey the area. Someone would yell, "Back it up!" to the crowd and I would echo them, "Okay, back it up!" The look, some attitude, and, with the occasional small talk, each security team assumed I was with the other.

I was doing well until the hotel's GM arrived. I couldn't let him see me. I'd stroll behind trees to hide without looking like I was hiding from security. The cast was loving this. Then the official horns blew. The procession was arriving and everyone scheduled to meet the royals got into line. I threw my clipboard behind a tree and stepped into line somewhere in the middle.

We were given proper protocol instructions that included not reaching out to her unless she did first and refer to her initially as "Your Majesty" followed by "Ma'am." "It's Ma'am as in Ham, not Mum as in Hum," they'd say. Or was it the other way around?

In walked the Prime Minister, The Queen, the Duke and a few other Sirs. It took a long time for anyone to reach the middle of the line. But then in her floral print dress, big hat, purse, and pearls, she was in front of me ... crystal blue eyes, alabaster skin (not sure what that means ... pure and pasty?), a gentle smile and about a foot and a half away. I was so close I could have easily slapped her.

But what do you say to the Queen? "How are the kids?" "What's in the purse?" "Is that your scepter or are you just happy to see me?" One of my comic friends suggested, "Keep movin' sister there's only room for one queen here!"

Our chat began like this:

QEII
Hello. What do you do here?
ME
Well, your Majesty, I am an entertainer here at the hotel.
QEII
Oh? What do you do?
ME
I am a ventriloquist.

QEII

Oh! (Chuckle) Do you know (*Insert British ventriloquist here*)?

ME

Yes I do! (I did not. Is lying to the Queen a criminal offense?)

Some of my Brit friends could care less about the Royal family but we do not have this kind of thing in the US so I was excited. But at this point I had gotten what I came for and now I was ready for her to move on down the receiving line. However, "Lengthy Lizzi" had other plans.

QEII:

Well thank you for bringing your craft to the Commonwealth.

ME:

It's my pleasure Ma'am.

QEII:

It's lovely what they have done to the property isn't it?

ME:

It is ...

I should mention that she has now spent more time with me than the general manager or anyone else. The GM was shocked I was there, but what could he do now?

It's a very impressive skill to make a stranger feel relaxed by acting interested and making small talk. The Queen had to do it for twenty to thirty people at this stop in the day and probably 100 more times before the day was through.

She continued with me a bit more and, to wrap it up, I repeated something I heard someone else say earlier, referring to a wrist brace she wore from an incident with a horse.

ME:

... And might I add, (gesturing to the brace) you're looking quite well.

QEII:

Thank you. I am feeling much better.

Her Majesty moved on down the line. The chat lasted about three minutes, which gave the press time to push in on us and get some good shots. I was hoping to get a copy of a photo or two from the local press. I mean, you can't just put your arm around her and snap a shot with your disposable camera! (Ben Affleck, maybe; the Queen, NEVER...)

But the fun wasn't over yet. Next was the Duke. He has always been known for his "green" agenda but, as a person, is thought of by some as a bit of a dud. I really just wanted to leave at this point but there were herds of people behind me. And when it comes to a receiving line with royalty, there is no way out until it is over.

Phillip got to the girl next to me and, in an attempt at small talk, he leaned in and read her badge out loud. "Executive confidential secretary. To whom are you the secretary for?" To which I leaned in and said, "I believe that's confidential!" I thought it was hilarious. He was not amused.

Two hours later I was back in my apartment when the phone rang. I was asked to participate in the evening's royal performance. I was in a panic. It is a once in a lifetime thing, but my act was still very young and crude ... to be blunt, a lot of dick jokes. It would only be a few minutes of time though, so I agreed.

Basically I had three jokes that I stretched. I remember very little about it. It was kinda like the first time you have sex: dark, scary, and over before it started.

Later, the Prime Minister asked me if I would come perform at his mansion Christmas Day where he hosts the children's orphanage. I did and afterwards, he asked if there was anything he could do for me while on the island. I explained that the building I was staying at was new and had telephones, but the road had no telephone lines. The next day, my phone had a dial tone.

But there's an update to this story.

In 2012 when doing technical work in Los Angeles (See: The Beverly Hilton), I was asked to be the exclusive handheld cameraman for Prince William and Kate's participation at a technology summit. They were coming to the States right after the wedding. One of the production teams thought it would be cute to paste the photo of the Queen and me on the back of my press pass. I was inches from them both for about forty minutes. William noticed the photo and asked if that was his grandmother! I peeked out from behind the camera and gave the thumbs up since I was supposed to be "invisible and unobtrusive."

He was engaging, incredibly charming, and showed tremendous humility to each person he addressed as if they were the only people in the room.

Blackmailing Trump's
Entertainment Director

Atlantic City Casinos were a hot spot for entertainment through the mid '70s until the late '90s. I built a good name and got many opportunities there as an opening act, a comedy club comic, and as a comedy guest star of the big singer/dancer revue shows. I also worked for "The Donald" several times.

The first time was to perform on his 282 foot yacht. There was a friggin' helicopter on top. It was his birthday bash and I did twenty minutes along with a few other acts including Fred Travalena and Sandy Duncan. Weird. Later, I headlined a few of his revue shows, hosted some casino game shows, and performed at his Hawaiian Tropics Pageant.

I was playing The Comedy Stop at the Tropicana when I get a call from the people at (then called) Trump's Castle. At that time the casino had a show playing called "Freddie Roman Live," which had a *Tonight Show* format with guests, a couch, and was hosted by Catskills/Friars' comedian Freddie Roman. That night, their headlining guest was to be Jerry Van Dyke, brother of Dick Van Dyke, who had finally made his mark in show business when he won an Emmy for playing Luther Van Dam on ABC's *Coach* with Craig T. Nelson.

Apparently Jerry was stuck in the snow coming down from Boston and it was very close to show time. Trump wanted me to fill in. They offered to send a car for me so, when I got off stage after the Trop's first show, I'd be carted over to do show number one for Freddie Roman, then back and forth for show number two.

I agreed and shared the information with the other club

comics. The night's headliner said that I should get Jerry Van Dyke's paycheck. This planted a seed on the limo ride over. Do I have the balls to ask? Will they ever call me again? If they say *no*, do I stay and make some money anyway? If I leave, it's found money I wasn't expecting.

I arrive backstage and the show is already underway. I am quietly greeted by the stage manager, who immediately grabs my show trunk and music, and the entertainment director who shakes my hand and thanks me for coming.

The wardrobe mistress is ironing my jacket and de-linting me from the car ride. I'm being mic'd when the director asks, "So, what do you want to for the gig?" I reply, "Well, I want what Jerry Van Dyke was going to get."

He laughs. "I can't do that."

"Why not? You're asking me to handle the spot and the check is cut already."

"I can't."

I pause and say, "Okay. Well, I understand. Thanks for the call and I hope we get to work together again soon. I love your guys." I turn and start packing up.

Five minutes later, the stage manager walks up to me. "Michael, the ED, says it's handled and you're good."

I did the show, got a check for an amount I've never seen prior or since, and I never worked at that casino again! But to be fair, they changed their entertainment format to bands, so in the back of my mind, I take a little credit for no future bookings. I have seen that director in recent years and we are very happy to have a drink and a laugh.

Oh. That headlining comic at the Trop that planted the seed was Ray Romano.

A few years later Jerry and I did a New Year's Eve show together for Trump. Jerry was so sweet and his family was beautiful.

It is widely known that, for years, Jerry had great disdain for his brother's success. The funniest thing he did in his act was after a big voiceover introduction of his credits, the band would play him on with the theme song from *The Dick Van Dyke Show*. Jerry would turn red and throw a tantrum like a five-year-old with, "Oh come on!" then storm off stage until the band had to coax him back on. He knew he would never step out from his big brother's shadow and only now was he okay having fun with it.

A Favor For The Mob Boss

It was around 1998 and I thought I was going to retire the act and find a new career when I got a call for a summer gig headlining a new show in Atlantic City. I decided to write some new material and go out with a bang. One last gig.

From that job I was awarded "Act of the Year" by the staple publication, *Atlantic City Magazine* (got a plaque and everything!) and Chuck Darrow, who, I was told, was the meanest, toughest entertainment critic, gave me rave reviews. I also gained a new fan...

Notorious mob boss, "Little" Nicky Scarfo, who took over for his father, Nikki Sr. when he went to prison, came to see the show almost every weekend. And every weekend, he would expect me to come say hello after the show. One night, after a particularly bad night due to a combination of the power going out twice mid-show and a violent drunk in the audience, I wearily walked to my dressing room where I found a young waiter from the steakhouse restaurant, which should have been closed an hour earlier.

"Excuse me, Mr. Scarfo is in the steakhouse and has requested you come say hello," the waiter said.

Saturated and tired of being "on" I replied, "Please tell Mr. Scarfo I appreciate that but it's been a very tough night and I'll look forward to seeing him next weekend."

"He told me not to return without you."

Who knows what that meant?

"....Okay, give me a minute to clean up." I made myself look presentable and was escorted through the back hallways and into the restaurant. Sure enough, it had been closed for two hours, but the wait staff was standing by tableside for Little

Nicky and his guests.

ME:

Mr. Scarfo, good to see you again.

NS:

Michael, I'd like to introduce you to my son and our good family friends, the Espositos. I was hoping you'd do some comedy for my guests since they didn't get a chance to see you in the show.

ME:

I appreciate that but you know comedy is never funny for four people and a line of kitchen staff.

NS:

Please. It would be a personal favor to me, and I'd take care of you for your time.

ME:

No, no, it's not about that. It's been a terribly long night and...

NS:

Please.

So what was I gonna do? Say no and leave? I was on the spot. I couldn't give a good enough reason and he wasn't going to stop asking. So I brought a puppet up and began. When I thought it was getting quiet, I started laying into the wait staff, which got some laughs.

Six minutes later, I thanked them and, with a four person round of applause, Nicky thanked me, slipped something into my breast pocket, and I left. I didn't dare look at the gift until I was in my dressing room. It was a $900 tip. The cheap bastard couldn't have made it an even grand?

Michael J. Fox Screwed Me

I have been to the *Late Show with David Letterman* theater twice. The first was as an audience member, which was great. While in line, the audience producers give some direction about what works and what doesn't on camera. For instance, clapping and laughing is picked up well in the microphones. But "whooing" does not. The frequency just sounds ugly on air.

The pre-show warm-up for the audience is unlike any other show. Long time warm up comic, Eddie Brill hosts a show all his own with Letterman highlight clips, music, and then introduces Paul and the Band, who come out and play a few songs. It's like a fast-paced rock concert.

The audience is wired when, out of nowhere, about three minutes to show time, Dave walks out without a jacket. Everyone loses their shit. He laughs and casually leans against a camera right over the front row and starts chatting about anything and everything on his mind. Then he says, "Okay we're gonna start. Have a good time and I'll see you in a minute." The opening theme starts and a minute later he walks out with his jacket on and we already feel like we know him personally.

The second time I went to the Ed Sullivan Theater was as a "plant" in the front row. I had been called a day prior to perform in a sketch. We rehearsed with the producer around 4:00 p.m. on show day, two hours before the audience was let in.

My bit was scheduled for segment two. But Michael J. Fox's segment was going long, because he was updating everyone on his Parkinson's disease. I was told to sit tight as they planned to move things around to insert the sketch in segment three.

After another segment ended, it was clear I was bumped and Michael J. Fox was still droning on.

Jesus Christ. I'm sitting there thinking, "You were diagnosed like fifteen years ago! WE KNOW! What about my bit, you sonofabitch!" For the record, I like Michael J. Fox very much.

I sold a few jokes and Top Ten lists to Letterman. But I was never working in the offices. Like many comics not on staff, my material had to be faxed in. I watched the jokes being done while at home like everyone else.

I did learn a few things while on the inside. Self-admittedly not being in the comedy scene for years, Dave has allegedly developed a weird philosophy on what works and what doesn't. For instance, he doesn't want Canadians on the main floor of the theater because he had a bad experience once and feels they don't "get" him. Buddy Hackett did that too. He had the box office seat the audience based on age and background demographics that he pre-determined.

I haven't enjoyed Dave for quite a few years now. But I check in here and there out of loyalty. When he was putting cameras on monkeys, dressing Oscar winning actors in bunny suits, or interrupting live broadcasts in adjacent studios, I was in love with him. In recent years, he's just phoned it in and developed this "lame duck" persona that used to be funny when a joke didn't fly. Now all the jokes are set up that way. He has, however, become a terrific interviewer when he's truly interested.

So in closing, Michael J. Fox still has Parkinson's.

Mother Nature

Traveling the world, I have been in blizzards, tornados, and in 1995, in the middle of Hurricane Felix.

I had signed a six month job in Bermuda when, in month four, the international weather service announced a hurricane was coming towards the tiny island, and it was going to be big.

The tourists, along with my cast, were evacuated. However I could not get a flight out in time. I was living in the hotel so I and the staff boarded up doors and taped "X's" on the huge windows so, in case they broke, it would only be in a few pieces as opposed to thousands of shards. The engineer also determined the safest rooms for us to weather the storm.

The sky went black very quickly, the winds were screaming and the power went out. In a matter of hours, flagpoles were ripping out of the ground, flying through windows, and trees were falling through rooftops. It was relentless.

I am huddled in a tiny hotel room with the general manager when the phone rings. All switchboard calls were transferred to this phone.

CALLER
Hi! This is Amanda from Rosenbluth Travel confirming my client's reservation this morning!
ME
Do you live in a bubble? There's a hurricane here! Turn on the news. We've evacuated!
CALLER
Well can I speak to someone in reservations please?
ME
It's 3:00 a.m. There's no one here but the skeleton crew.

CALLER
And who would that be?
ME
... The general manager, the head chef, the engineer and the ventriloquist!

I slam the phone down.

Maybe forty-eight hours later, the hurricane reduced to a rain. I was told the tiny stone bridge connecting the main land of the island to the airport was gone and it could be days before I'd get to go home. The hotel interior was in pretty good shape but still no power. So for the next few days the chef made everything in the kitchen before it spoiled. We ate like kings and opened the bar to never ending "Dark & Stormys."

The producers of my show emailed me to try and sell off the set and make sure their equipment was on high ground before I left the island. I was going stir crazy and somehow had not been called by the airlines when the first flight had come in and left.

Thanks to my two good friends on the police force (both named Kevin), I got a call around 7:00 p.m. "We heard on the police radio, an American Airlines flight is coming in at 9:30 p.m. Get your bags together. We're coming to get you."

By the way — I survived.

Joan Rivers & Mink;
Frank Gorshin & Drink

I had already heard Bill Cosby's albums. At camp some kids played Cheech and Chong and the live recordings of college bar piano player, John Valby's rated R song parodies. One day I was flipping through the record store's cassettes in the comedy section when I saw a cover with a blond woman wearing a mink stole and bright red lipstick. The album title, "What Becomes a Semi-Legend Most." The stamp next to the title said "ADULT CONTENT — Parental Discretion Advised."

I bought it, ran home, locked the door to my room, tore open the cassette box, slammed it into the boom box (it was the '80s), put on my headphones (the size of toasters) and pressed play. I was stunned. Dumbfounded. Numb. Not from the comedic content. I didn't understand half of what the hell this woman was talking about, but the crowd.

The wall of laughter was like a tidal wave over and over. I had never heard anything like this before. I listened to the tape ten times a day. I studied it: the timing, the vocal dynamics, the audience ups and downs, the insults, and the zingers. The balancing act of insult, then appeasement and compassion only to club someone over the head a second time! I was hooked. When I was a kid, it was Abbott and Costello. But this was something completely different. Live. Organic. Over the years, I'd studied and appreciated all genres of comedy. Whether it's my kind of comedy or not, I get it.

It's a shame people today only reference Joan Rivers for her crass, red carpet chatter, and plastic surgery. They have no idea that even with Moms Mabley, Phyllis Diller, and Totie

Fields, Joan was the trailblazer for comediennes and comics across the board.

I was first introduced to Joan through Clint Holmes, the musical director of her late night show on the brand new FOX network, scandalously going up against Johnny Carson. Clint later became a tremendous talent all his own.

I had the opportunity to open for Joan a few times over the years. It was difficult to be comfortable with her because each time I'd open, I'd have to reacquaint myself with her all over again. It generally took a few days. I make a point of never talking shop with stars. I try to disarm them on a more personal level of chat ... family, food, clothing.

Most of the time Joan would rarely be in one place long enough to engage deeply. But I knew I was "in" when we were in Minnesota and she popped her head in my dressing room after walking off stage asking, "Were they weird for you?" I replied, "So weird the whole set."

"Good, I knew it wasn't me."

I learned early on that sometimes it's not the artist that's crazy and rude but the entourage that tries to cater and protect them. I think the first time I opened for Joan I was standing in the wing ready to go on when her handler said, with all seriousness, "Don't do better than her." ... *Ew!*

It's fascinating that Joan, Rickles, Diller, even the younger Bette Midler were all cut from the same cloth. No matter how much they have done or how much they have in the bank, they are all worried that tomorrow the call won't come in and they'll go under. It is The Depression mentality. There are no coat tails to ride on when it comes to these people because they feel they have none.

Secondly, unlike the stars of today, these people don't have an entourage of reps. Maybe there is one assistant traveling with them, mainly due to their age. Little ego, they just want to work, period.

A perfect example is Frank Gorshin.

In today's comedy scene you don't see a lot of variety acts as household names: magicians, jugglers, impressionists, only ventriloquist Jeff Dunham has been able to semi-integrate. But in the impressionist world, before guys named Danny Gans,

Fred Travalena, or Rich Little, there was Frank Gorshin, most noted for his role as "The Riddler" in the 1960s *Batman* TV series, and the voice of many characters in the stop motion, *Rudolf the Red Nosed Reindeer* holiday film.

Frank had appeared on every major talk and variety show for twenty years. In the '90s a musical revue show was created around him. His character impressions would appear scene to scene and he would then have a formal comedy segment in the show to feature his act. Even with his dentures whistling on stage and incessant cigarette smoking (he loved smoking), he was still very good and pulled in an audience.

But Frank didn't always show up for the curtain call. The cast of ten would bow for the closing number and rev up for a big entrance from the star of the show, the man whose name is on the billboard. They'd announce Frank, point to the wing and three out of seven times Frank wouldn't come out. The co-stars were quality, seasoned professionals and they were getting pissed.

Finally, I knocked on his dressing room door, walked in and found Frank on the couch with his head in his hands. I said, "So Frank ... what's goin' on?" He went on a tirade full of embarrassment, guilt, and humiliation. He hadn't felt he "got" the audience. He hadn't lived up to the level of show he felt they expected and deserved from him and he just couldn't go out and face them. He didn't deserve the bow. What we thought was ego turned out to be the very self-loathing and fear of rejection that almost every comic has from their earliest days. Did they like me? Was I funny? How do I compare? They're judging my guts.

Of course he then buttoned it with, "...and the other thing is, I dunno, Mikey ... maybe I shouldn't drink so much before the show." He loved his booze as much as his cigs.

A year later Frank starred on Broadway as George Burns to rave reviews. He died not long after.

I Started Out In Blacks

The only thing that got me through high school was the work/study program. A senior program that I started doing as a freshman after strong-arming Mrs. Miesse (mee-see), the school guidance counselor.

Most kids would go into Vo-Tech but I interned in TV production. (See: KYW-TV) The deal was, no job, back to class. So, when my station contract ended in my senior year, I applied and was rejected by every mall job available.

B. DALTON BOOK MANAGER:
What was the last book you read?
ME:
Errr ... Entertainment Weekly? ... Juggs?

Maybe I'll just go see if Cinnabon is hiring.

My soon to be, great friend known as "John O" told me about a stage tech gig at what was once an amazing dinner theater tucked away in Valley Forge, Pennsylvania and home to flashy, exciting Las Vegas-style revue shows.

There I learned the craft of theater production that later took me around the world. But while I was there I became a staple. Honing my skills in the 560-seat theater as spot op, fly rail crew, stage management, and eventually sound engineer. I had excellent timing, common sense, and did my best work during emergencies.

John O. and I were known as "wind and rewind" — the comedy duo of the theater. John had amazing ethics, character, and smarts, and was as dry witted, snarky, and silly as myself. Many nights after the show we would sit on our cars for hours after the show, recounting events and laughing so hard we'd roll around peeing ourselves until security would come by to make sure we were okay.

We took our goofing off as seriously as our work. So when a cast member or two would attempt to play tricks on us, we came up with some brilliant moments:

The dancers wore black leather bra and g-string costumes. We took artist charcoal and colored in their bras so when they took them off, their boobs were black for the rest of the show.

We bought a Hallmark card that beeped "Happy Birthday," removed the mechanism and mounted it inside one of the showgirl's headdresses. Activating it as she walked out on stage, only she could hear it and it was super loud against her cranium. Her eyes went wide and she was completely out of step with the other dancers. Everyone thought she was nuts.

During an ice skating adagio, we cut out a black circle of duvetyn (curtain), laid it on the ice and pretended to ice fish in the middle of the production number.

Tons of known, unknowns, and *a lot* of has-beens came through Valley Forge:

We had the "Stars of the Lawrence Welk Show." All the deadbeat, poor, over forty-five year old cast members that grumbled at the thought of Lawrence in Palm Springs lounging in luxury even after his Parkinson's set in. The show was hosted by Dick Dale, a six foot tall, tux-wearing gentleman with low knees. What I mean is, his knees looked lower on his legs than normal so when he bent, he looked like he was on stilts. There was also Ava Barber: not overweight but a big-boned lady who wore a lot of beige. And the crew's favorite, Joe Feeney: 5'0", green tux, and sang everything from "Mariah" to "Greatest Love" in an operatic voice. They traveled cross-country in a VW Bus, sold eight-track tapes and always filled the house.

We had Loreen Yarnell of the famed mime team Shields & Yarnell, who was the stereotypical, flighty, 1970s beatnik actress. She was fired after she ended her eighteen-minute set ten minutes early, walking off stage and leaving it empty. Her reason? "It just felt right." Ummm, not to the twelve naked cast members in the lower dressing rooms with the closing number starting without them.

And from *Eight is Enough*, *Happy Days*, and *American Graffiti*, Susan Richardson, who on press night, deviated from the script of a fun rock & roll revue show to talk about apartheid, her abortion, and to introduce her gynecologist in the audience. It was alleged that her doctor was paid off by the producers to tell her she could no longer physically do the show, rather than paying a huge firing fee.

I have always kept my stage blacks (shirt, pants & shoes) and tool bag. It all certainly prepared me for the future.

Japan Didn't Have Mac & Cheese

This was gonna be the first time I had traveled internationally. I was offered a comedy spot within a show produced at the Show Boat Casino in Tokyo, Japan.

Of course, I didn't speak Japanese, so they translated eight minutes of my act and sent me the cassette to learn and memorize it phonetically. (That's right, cassette).

My concern was that, if there was any audience heckling, I wouldn't be able to respond. Turned out, that wasn't going to be a problem.

Ninety-eight percent of the audiences were Japanese businessmen who never actually watched the show, until the topless American dancers were on. Otherwise, they spoke business, rarely looking up.

As a customer courtesy, the dancers were generally asked to sit with the men after the show (clothed). They were rarely spoken to, mainly out of protocol, but also because neither gender was bilingual. The first night, the girls decided they were ready to leave. They stood, said goodbye, and the businessmen handed them money. A lot of money.

At first the girls were offended thinking they were being called hookers, until the house manager came to explain it was a sign of prosperity, and to refuse would be an insult. One night the female singer was given a mink stole. For the record, the ventriloquist didn't get shit. (Sure, I wasn't bilingual or female, but I would have sat with them topless.) I did, however, receive an offer to do a guest spot on a network television soap opera.

I was invited to make a cameo on their version of *General Hospital*. I had no lines, nor did I have anything to do in the scene. Basically I was asked to walk across the shot, past the hospital front desk as the actors were speaking. A title graphic appeared on screen that read, "American comedian, Michael Ziegfeld." Why? Who knows? I guess anything American is considered awesome regardless of it making any sense.

I was only around twenty years old and my culinary palate was less than mature. I was young, making a modest income as a road comic, happily, and regularly eating macaroni and cheese as a staple meal.

The first week we were in Japan, the cast and production team were nightly diplomatic guests at a round table dinner full of politicians and business executives. Every night it was the same thing: fish parts, octopus with the big jelly head, calamari. (Not the fried kind, but the kind that looks and chews like a condom just out of the wrapper. Don't ask how I know that.)

I couldn't eat it. I hated all seafood at the time, let alone sushi. So for days I ate nothing but noodles or rice until the last night of the week, when the translator said, "Oh, you will be most happy! Tonight is 'Western' themed menu!" I said, "Oh great! Western night!" Turns out, it was the same food, but with *forks*.

As a side note, mac & cheese was not a product sold in Japan. The producer shipped me a case of it that took up most of my tiny apartment.

I've been to over fifty countries now. You know it's time to stop traveling when people ask, "Hey, have you ever been to Civitavecchia?" and you reply, "Probably."

Literally Breaking Into Show Business
(and The Offices of Don Buchwald, Rosie O'Donnell And Lorne Michaels)

I was fourteen and skipped morning high school classes to be in the studio audience of *People Are Talking* at KYW-TV3 — Philadelphia.

Television really turned me on at a very young age. So after giving myself the unofficial tour of the station (See: KYW-TV), a few years later, I became the youngest intern/P.A. at an NBC affiliate. (KYW is now a CBS o/o station.)

And so began a pattern...

The New York Break-Ins:

Around 2003, I was living in New York when I came up with my first television idea called "The Tomato Lounge." It was a huge undertaking. Three days, three locations, ten-hour days, four principle actors, twenty extras, musical numbers, and more. But how would I get the materials seen with no representation?

Step One: Make the packaging original so it would not be lost in the piles of unsolicited submissions. Instead of the usual Fed/Ex packaging, we built huge foam tomatoes on platters. The delivery sheet was a supermarket receipt. You opened the top of the tomato and the pitch book and VHS tape was inside.

Step Two: I dressed up like one of the countless couriers in town. Grungy, haggard, annoyed, and, to complete the ensemble, I had my photoshopped ID badge from Courier Express. (There is no such company that I know of.) A friend dropped me off. I walked to security, glanced at my clipboard of fake signatures and said, "Yeah. Bill Jensen, William-Morris?"

GUARD:
Okay, we'll take it.
ME:
Sorry, someone has to sign for it from his office.
GUARD:
Hey, this is William-Morris!
ME:
Congratulations. I'm Courier Express. I have seven more stops to make today. Either they come down or one of you takes me up. Let's go.

I realized that if I were a person that had no interest in show business, I wouldn't give two shits who they were. Hell, it's only television for God's sake.

Minutes later they unlocked the elevator and sent me up to the fortieth floor. I walked in, gave a tired salutation to the receptionist and handed her the clipboard to sign. As I turned around to leave, I heard her on the intercom. "Mr. Jenson? There is a giant tomato out here for you. No, not a real one ... I think you should come out here."

I have photographed documentation of this event. I got a meeting the next week. And no, they never knew I was the same guy who made the delivery.

Over the next month, I played courier to numerous other high-powered stars, agents, and producers. When security was locked tight, good timing helped. It got me into Lorne Michaels' office thanks to the distraction of a fire alarm at NBC: the secretary was nowhere to be found when I dropped one on the desk of Rosie O'Donnell, but only after workin' the magic to dig up their new, unlisted company address. (I later performed for her "Rosie's Broadway Kids" program.)

I was close to being caught only once, and forty percent of my efforts got returned calls.

The L.A. Break-Ins, Part I:

When I moved to Los Angeles I had very few contacts for getting pitch meetings with networks. Not to mention the fact that receptionists and assistants hate talking to "the general public." However, assistants do like to talk to other assistants.

So I called pretending to be my own assistant, explaining that "Michael Ziegfeld is going to be in town until next Thursday rolling out new content and he has specifically asked to meet with Bob*, so I wanted to see how we can get their calendars together." Of course she asked what it was about but, as a lowly assistant, I would not be privy to such things. "However, it's extremely time sensitive." She would request an email to forward and I'd send the same general information with a company website and legitimate six degrees of separation.

Seventy percent of the time, I got meetings.

Let me warn you Newbies: My partner and I had the website, packaging, and credits to back up a decent worthy meeting. We also created a very specific way of presenting our communication and product via electronic press kits or in person and made sure we knew the likes and dislikes of these people regarding pitches. A bad move can hurt you. I crashed and burned once or twice. But that's another story in a book I'm planning to bury...

Okay, one more break-in for ya.

In general, you can't just call up a network or agency and ask, "Hey! Who's in charge of development and can you connect me?" It is the same with huge agencies. If you don't have a name, you don't get through the switchboard.

So when I had to figure out who represented television at a major agency, I Googled them only to find a single agent's name from the publishing department who had been interviewed for some college paper. So I thought, "Okay, what's a big publishing company the big boys deal with?" And then I made the call.

RING RING.
ASSISTANT: Virginia Sandford's office. This is Rebecca.
ME: Hey, Rebecca. It's Michael from Simon & Schuster.
ASSISTANT: Oh, hi Michael!
ME: Listen. I have this package on my desk and I don't know what to do with it so I thought I'd send it your way. It's a TV thing. Who over there should it go to?
ASSISTANT: Oh, send it to Bob Baker in television, extension 5923.

ME:Okay, thanks. Have a good day.
ASSISTANT: You too.
RING RING
BOB: Bob Baker.
ME: Hi, Bob. This is (fake name.) I was referred to you by Virginia Sandford.
BOB: Oh, sure. What can I do for you?

Voila! Now of course Rebecca had no idea who I was. But she knew I sounded calm, casual, and familiar and she knew who Simon and Schuster was. She probably assumed she forgot who I was because of a heavy workload and a high-strung boss.

RING RING.
MZ: Hello?
DAD: Hi, how's it going?
MZ: Okay. How are you?
DAD: Good. What've you been up to today?
MZ: Lying and pretending to be different people. I'm exhausted.

Some might say I was merely acting, pulling innocent bystanders into my improvisation! Yet again, with my accomplice, AT&T, I broke into another busy avenue of show business.

It had been several years. My career was going fine, but when I moved to LA to look for new management, one who could handle my literary and performing works under one roof, I had considered rejoining the ranks of "Courier Express."

That day in Philadelphia was a slippery slope. Please kids: Do not attend morning talk shows in local markets. Or to put it another way: This is your brain, this is your brain on show business...

* Names have been changed to protect the innocent.

The L.A. Break -Ins, Part II:

It was the TCA Press Junket at the Beverly Hilton Hotel.

Every day for two weeks a different television network introduces their new shows to the reporting, reviewing, and blogging media, which includes a Q&A of the cast and executive producers. If one could get in, it would mean unprecedented access to every current "player" under one roof.

I decided, hey, if I could get myself press passes to the Grammys when I was seventeen years old (See: The Grammy Award), then at the experienced age of twenty-two, I could get into this place.

It had been a tough summer financially but I dipped into my dwindling bank account to make 100 press kits for my literary works. The kit would be on a one-gig thumb drive and the price included two-sided printing; one with my logo and the other with a web address to the same material for those who were virus-paranoid about plugging something into their computer. It also included pre-loaded data files for Mac and PC users (harder than you think); and a lanyard. Instead of handing over a ratty old business card or a huge package of material, this would be an easy, novel, and subtle marketing tool to pass along.

But how would I get it to them? I didn't know the physical access the press would have. Maybe there would be some gift swag bags I could sneak the thumb drives into. But there was no guarantee the VIPs would get 'em or see 'em.

Thank God, after the panel Q&As, the press would go up on stage. While they swarmed the stars, I'd approach the show runners and executive producers.

The confrontation is a precise formula of vocabulary. It has to be part ego-stroking for them to feel flattered but not so much as to make you feel or be subservient. You don't want to lessen your persona of value. It has to be charismatic without making them feel trapped. You must ask permission to give them something while making sure that they take it. If possible, you should execute this plan twice in case one member of the show loses it, breaks it, or throws it away.

Breaking Down My Script and the Psychology:
"John. Hi, I'm Michael Paul..." {*Get focused attention, then warmth and human connection.*}

"I am writing on another show..." {*Industry legitimacy and not one of the millions of wannabes.*}

"...but I specifically came here today to meet you." {*flattery and put on a pedestal.*}

"I want to work for you." {*Direct, concise, sincere.*}

"I know this isn't the ideal moment, but would you allow me to give you my press kit." {*Asking permission to enter their personal space*}

You'll notice I did not punctuate that last sentence like a question even though it clearly is one. That is because I asked it in a tone where "no" was not an option in their reply, firm but kind, with none of the communication being weighed down with a lot of fluff or detail. These people are busy, inundated, and don't want to feel used by people. This all must be accomplished literally in *ten seconds* without being discovered by the people running the event.

You see, everyone assumes you're with someone else. The network thinks you're with the hotel. The talent thinks you're with the press. The press thinks you're with the network (And your friends think you're with the insane...) But you have to have a personality that can morph with confidence when it's time to blend in or be aggressive and shut someone down who's questioning your legitimacy.

This happened:

EX.1)
NETWORK PERSON: Can I help you?
ME: No.
NETWORK PERSON: Well, who are you?
ME: I am with the hotel and you are in a secure area. Who are you?

Then she backs off. I get nice. I smile and banter with her as an equal being on the "same team" and she leaves.

EX. 2)
I was trying to speak to a show runner / EP when her business partner stepped in.

PARTNER: I'm sorry, are you an actor or something?
(Not missing a beat I reply, a tad annoyed or insulted)
ME: No. I am with The Huffington Post.
PARTNER: Oh, I'm sorry. I missed that part!
(To warm the EP up again, I turn back to her.)

ME: ... The sensibility of your project choices have been amazing and this show is completely your voice!

EP: Oh my God. Thank you! Of course, I'd love to take your press kit.

I only approached the people I truly felt respect, appreciation, and creative connection to. While I talk about how to speak to a person, it is by no means false. Nor am I saying these people are shallow or easily manipulated. All human beings need to be spoken to in a certain way to hear and be heard. I just figured out how to do that in a matter of minutes. If they hadn't sensed my sincerity, it wouldn't have worked.

I attended six days of the event and handed out at least twenty thumb drives. Only two people didn't want to take them, instead asking me to call their office assistants, one of whom gave me her name and direct number.

Did all of this "007" effort work? Time will tell.

Jim Henson & The Workshop

This book would be incomplete without mentioning my time with certain branches of the Jim Henson Company. I had wonderful, engaging experiences with Richard Hunt, probably due to the fact that he always took a liking to young, Jewish looking boys. I had numerous encounters with Jane Henson who was also a very generous fan of mine. She was at all of my auditions and some projects, each time turning to others to say, "He reminds me of Frank." Of course referring to Frank Oz.

One day in the late '80s/early '90s, I was on the back lot studio tour of MGM Studios — Florida, when the tramcar announcer said, "And to our left are studio production offices currently being rented by Jim Henson Productions."

I told my family I'd meet them at the end of the tour, leapt off the moving tram, climbed under a fence, and walked into the front office. I told the receptionist, "I'm here to see Jim Henson." She said he wasn't in and as I turned to leave, the Muppet creator entered, conversing with another man. When he finished, I introduced myself and told him I was going to work with him when I was old enough. He told me he looked forward to that day and wrote down his address for me to write him. I still have the note.

I went up to help on multiple projects in the New York headquarters, home to the workshop, and a few blocks away in The Carriage House, their original building during the early days of pre-*Sesame Street*. It's one of the only original properties the Henson kids still own.

There was a period of time where I put away the puppets for a while. Amongst other things, it wasn't helping my social life. But of course, as a first love, it has always returned.

In 1992, I was in the finals for *"The Tonight Show* Comedy Challenge,"* a gimmick to boost ratings the year after Jay Leno took the chair from Johnny Carson. After my set, a woman approached me and handed me a business card. The man she worked for wanted to help me, and she suggested I call him that week.

The man was Arthur Novell, a hugely respected name in show business PR and marketing. He also represented everything Jim Henson did. I took a train to New York and met him at the 21 Club. I could smell the old money and power in the room.

It was Arthur and Carroll Spinney, the original Big Bird and Oscar the Grouch, with whom I'd had a long-time correspondence (for novices, these performers do the voice *and* the manipulation of the character), who called me when The Muppets were holding a very rare workshop in Los Angeles.

The Muppet Workshops were a week long testing and training ground for prospective Muppeteers. There are generally only a handful of slots available so there would be a series of auditions and callbacks done over a two day period.

At the time, I was performing at Harvey's Lake Tahoe for three months. I gave some excuse, found a replacement, and booked a flight and hotel room for the entire week in LA. I somehow just assumed I would make it through the auditions. I had been waiting for this since I was three. (See: Howdy Doody)

As I sat in the waiting room, many people seemed to know each other. The east and west coast puppeteers rarely interacted. Many in the room would play with the characters they brought. I always hated that. It was like trying to show off their skills (or lack of) to others, checking out the competition. Lame voices and bad puns. Blech. Exhibited this way, it's no wonder people cringe at art forms like this.

Remember the movie *Showgirls* with the chick from *Saved by the Bell*? There is a scene where she kicks the lead dancer down a flight of steps to take her place in the show. Puppeteers can be a lot like that. They'll smack talk you to the casting people or cut off your puppet's arms while you're in the bathroom. (Not to me, but it happens!)

I kept to myself until two ladies pointed to me and said, "Are you Michael Ziegfeld?"

Lee Armstrong (*Fraggle Rock*) and Kamela Portuges (*Being John Malkovich*) had built a remote controlled talking sandwich for my stage show a few years earlier. We never met, only called and faxed through the process. They were awesome and also pulled me into their circle of friends.

The auditions were primarily led by *Sesame Street* puppet captain, Kevin Clash, creator of Muppet phenom, Elmo. The auditions consisted of eye focus, mouth manipulation, and lip syncing.

Out of maybe 600 people, around twenty made it into the workshop, including Lee and Kam.

The week consisted of a lot of improv and sketch performance drills. I wasn't always teamed up with the most collaborative puppeteers. Some performers can be very selfish and instead of "playing tennis," they hog the ball.

However after a split moment of nerves, I shook them off and I truly shone that week. I came up with a catch phrase for my sketch's character that made everyone giggle to the point where another sketch group asked me to walk through and make a cameo in their scene.

In my experience, Kevin only spoke to you when there was a problem or correction, although he was nice when approached.

A year later Carroll brought me to *Sesame Street*, introduced me to executive producer, Michael Loman, and there ya go.

A few memories stick out ...

A child that was going to be on the show wandered into the studio, saw Big Bird without a head and went berserk. Carroll went out and worked his magic, of course. The kid is probably in therapy to this day.

Frank Oz, slowly moving away from this becoming a film director, was only coming in one week out of each season to shoot a ton of sketches and record audio loops. I was pulled in to "right hand" Cookie Monster. Frank slapped my left hand to his hip, pulled Cookie's right hand to the belly, turned to me and said in his "Bert" voice, "Just follow me and don't get artsy." After we got the take, he took off the puppet and tossed it to me like a doctor's scrubs, moving onto the next set.

My second day I was invited to play an "anything Muppet" or nowadays called a "whatnot" ... basically an extra with interchangeable parts. I was forewarned not to mess up my one line or get my head in the shot because it was the last shot of the day and everyone was sweaty and tired. Big Bird had won a movie festival. My line was, "So, Big Bird, what movie are you gonna do next?" With complete conviction the bird says, "*Turkey Porn*." Everyone breaks into hysterical laughter. I was so focused, not finding that line in my script, it took a moment to realize I was being screwed with. My puppet replied, "Screw this. I'm going to Barney." I got groans.

My time with the company was brief, primarily due to my naiveté about the business side of show business.

During that period, all the Henson shows were still in flux following Jim's death. And like any company ... this was a club. People that play with dolls have the same office water cooler talk, seductions, egos, and backstabbing as they do at Enron. Only in this case, it was complete irony being the very show that taught kids how to be nice. (Email me for the pilot television script titled, "Welcome to the Jungle.")

In my case, there was a confrontation with an egomaniacal, credit mongering puppeteer who planted negative seeds about me prior to my first day. Later he was never rehired for the very behaviors of which he falsely slandered me.

But the catalyst was when I had been accidentally privy to a series of events that were not for my eyes and ears nor the public's, which brought my immediate, unofficial blackballing. I am aware of what stories were told about me to legitimize their actions and although eventually, karma played a part in those individuals' self-demises, their successors carry a grudge torch.

I have no ill will. I had a smidgen of an experience most never even get. I am forever grateful and had such fondness for my mentors who were there during that time.

I was told often by those at both *Sesame* and *Muppets* that I had another art form that paid my bills, the comedy and writing. I believe those puppeteers (especially those with families to feed) who have committed to waiting on the stoop of Henson, Sesame, or Disney for years in the line of succession, hoping to receive any kind of breadcrumb, deserve the castings today.

For the most part, the people who are now the "inner circle" are warm, talented, kind artists. I support and applaud them in continuing a noble craft and that legacy.

Puppeteering remains one of my favorite art forms.

My First Movie:
David Wain & *The Ten*

David Wain may not be a name parents know but the kids definitely do as a founding member of the first MTV and then CBS improv group *Stella*, later renamed, *The State*. David's first movie *Wet, Hot, American Summer* starred every young 20s actor-turned-celeb including David Hyde-Pierce, Paul Rudd, Molly Shannon, Amy Poehler, and countless others. It was a slow-burn success that turned into a cult classic.

David's second big movie was titled *The Ten*: Ten comedy vignettes based on the Ten Commandments. I was called in to audition for it. My first movie and in a co-starring role, I was to play an office assistant by day and a horrible ventriloquist lounge act by night.

I am told that they saw every ventriloquist coast to coast, from the birthday party guys to Jeff Dunham. The casting problem was finding a vent that actually had some remote level of acting ability in the more serious scenes.

The audition scene I read was a "breakup" between the dummy and me. I ended the scene with the puppet gently grabbing my face, turning me to him and softly delivering the last line as we sadly gazed at each other.

I remember David, co-writer and actor, Ken Marino, executive producer Jon Stern (*Children's Hospital*) and the casting directors were holding their mouths. Shocked, freaked, thrilled ... I couldn't tell so I finally asked, "Was that close to what you were looking for?" They were happy and gave me very kind accolades.

Simultaneously, I was finishing a stint in Las Vegas when I

started getting dates on cruise ships. I was signed to perform for press week on a brand new cruise ship for one of the top lines. (I am probably not legally allowed to mention the name ... but call me and I'll whisper it to you.) I had done several inaugurals and it was nice to know I was considered a sure-fire act.

But I knew that I was going to receive a final callback from *The Ten* which would be in conflict with the dates on the ship. I really felt I was going to get the job. So I asked my agent to call the entertainment director to ask if they wouldn't mind giving the ship gig to someone else. It was my hope that, given my excellent track record, and the fact that we were giving them three weeks' notice — plenty of time considering bookers have hired or cancelled entertainers in a day's notice — they'd grant my request.

Within five minutes we received notice that the cruise line had cancelled fourteen scheduled dates for the summer, sending a message that if I cancelled on them, they'd cancel on me.

I worked before I knew this company existed and I would work after. Their tactic did not persuade me to keep the engagement. To my agent's credit, she put in a call conveying her thoughts, disgusted by their rash, unwarranted, childish behavior. I was proud of her. After all, she has to keep things nice for the agency and their other clients too. I am but one performer.

People don't understand or respect that when you work for yourself, you are creating a template that did not exist before. Scientist, singer, architect, comedian: you create the work, find the client, sell the work, do the work, then start all over again. You are also using a whip and a chair to make sure you are getting the best deal possible when all people want is the discount price.

POTENTIAL CLIENT:
Do you have a discount rate?
ME:
Yes but then I only tell half the joke.

Three weeks later, after I booked the movie and *the week* I was supposed to be on the now cancelled cruise ship job, I was sitting on my couch eating a bowl of Cap'n Crunch and watching CNN. A live news report from Port Canaveral, Florida announced that upon leaving the port, the very cruise ship I was to be on had listed, tilting fifteen degrees to one side, leaving 260 people with injuries and millions of dollars in damages.

Unbelievable, right? A month later the entertainment director called my agent for my availabilities again and all was right with the world. I mean, except for the 260 people on that boat.

Meanwhile, I would now have a co-starring credit in a movie with Winona Ryder, Liev Schreiber, Oliver Platt, Famke Janssen, Ron Silver, Jessica Alba, Adam Brody, Paul Rudd, John Hamm, Jason Sudeikis, Justin Theroux, and all of Wain's regulars from *The State* including Michael Ian Black, Michael Showalter, A.D. Miles (head writer for Jimmy Fallon), and the rest.

The ventriloquist character I played was supposed to be a bad cabaret act. I chose to perform it as a good puppeteer but a poor lip technician. In other words, my lips would move. I laughed when I heard rumors of other vents throughout the industry saying, "Why'd they hire him? He was a horrible ventriloquist!"

David and Ken were so fun and sweet and supportive throughout the shoot. Especially considering that I didn't have tons of experience. Fortunately, I was the one character in the film who got to play it straight (normal) because everyone else was so quirky. That helped.

I remember the day I was acting in a crack house scene. The set designers cleaned this warehouse from top to bottom only to put new dirt on the floors. "It's clean dirt," they assured me.

I tried a bit of the Stanislavki Technique by not talking to anyone all day. I listened to depressing music on my iPod to feel as worn and disturbed as possible. Fake it on the outside till it you feel it on the inside. In the end, everyone was still a better actor than me.

I was disappointed that some of the better acting moments

for me were cut out or put into a montage due to time. I was hoping they'd end up on the DVD extras but to no avail.

Janeane Garofalo and I shared a car a few times during the shoot. As the two stand-ups it allowed us to go into comedy soapbox tirades while everyone else listened and asked questions. This made me feel less of an outsider to the very quirky improv/acting style of humor that David and *The State* cast abided by.

Honestly, I never really got it. It's ironic, dry, sometimes pointless, child-like banter that rarely seems complete in its payoff. It's a structure all its own but their audiences love it.

I was invited to Sundance where I got to experience the film's viewing and purchase for distribution.

The movie had a very small distribution. I think the PR company thought there were so many names in it, the buzz would take care of the marketing. With the exception of those in the improv and sketch comedy scene, much of the general public never saw it come through their towns or even heard of it.

I had thought this might be my springboard. As a young, overly eager actor, I convinced the producers to issue me a few clips prior to the release date so I could book a new movie with it. The casting agent needed to see it immediately so I uploaded it to my MySpace page for them to view it, then I would remove it.

Within hours I got an angry call from the movie company. The link had spread on the World Wide Web. I felt awful. I had ruined a very positive experience with overzealous desperation, attempting to micromanage my career. Fortunately once the link was down, it cut off any Internet ties.

As previously mentioned, there was a period where I would shoot myself in the foot due to eagerness or panic or perhaps a lack of confidence in my legitimacy. But it was nothing a little therapy couldn't fix. I finally nipped that in the bud.

I always thought my actions kept me from being put on the DVD cover of *The Ten* as a punishment and probably from ever being called by that camp of people again for future projects.

Jeff Dunham's sister told me he also really wanted the role. Years later David directed, *Dinner with Schmucks* with a similar character. This time it went to Jeff.

I have been in communication with that team over the years. They are as warm and sweet as ever. David's movie credits now include *Wanderlust*, *Role Models*, and numerous others.

I also reached out to Jon Stern about the footage and voiced my regret. He said he didn't recall any of it! *Sheesh*!

One Offs

A late night drink at the Tribeca Hotel introducing Siegfried & Roy on my left, to Harvey Fierstein and the cast of *Hairspray* on my right...Walking with Morgan Freeman to the bathroom ...Sharing a first class flight with game show host, Bob Eubanks...Getting drunk with Fleetwood Mac...pretending I didn't know BBC's Judith Charmers (Britain's Robin Leach) until she flipped.

I never get star struck because they aren't curing cancer or teaching children or cooking me breakfast. Let's put it in perspective people.

Paul Rudd: Chill, fun, nice, everyday guy. We hung out at a cast house during Sundance watching a football game, eating sandwiches in the kitchen, talking about his kids and comedy. I also tapped him for guidance on improv during multiple takes and later he corresponded with me regarding hiring PR agents. And yes ladies, he is that cute in person.

The Mills Brothers: The Mills Brothers were one of the pioneers of rhythm and blues, famous for songs like "Bye Bye Blackbird," "Opus One," and "Glowworm." Doing the casino circuit I met them enough times to become casual friends. Donald, at ninety-two, was the last of the brothers. He traveled and performed with his son John, a chunky, balding, Caucasian. John's mother was white. So when the announcer said, "Ladies and gentleman, the world famous Mills Brothers!" the audience was like, "*Who's the white dude?*"

John told the stories while Don sat on a folding chair until the band started up. Then he'd stand, sing, and sound amazing, then sit back down. A year before Don died, I saw them one more time and was invited on stage to sing my favorite Mills

Brothers song, "Up a Lazy River" with them. Awesome.

Dick Clark: I had worked for Clark when he licensed *American Bandstand* as a touring show with a singer/dancer cast and occasionally a celebrity, musical guest star stepping in. I would co-host with scripted banter opposite a pre-recorded Clark on a projection screen. He would talk about the year and the music, then "turn to me." I'd reply to the video, "That's right Dick!" (I know … I know.) Later, I was the host of *The American Music Awards Live* — the last twenty-five years of AMA music winners. It was cute until Christmas came. The hotel wanted a holiday theme and it became, *The AMAs On Ice* … awful. The kind of thing people tease about.

Dick was nice but a notorious penny pincher. When they went to record his video interstitials for the stage show at his office, he asked the independent video company to keep shooting so he could run off some teasers he needed for something else! He then asked for the tapes, footage, and time for free.

I will say, it was warming to see how his wife took care of him on the road. He traveled with a tiny roller bag. I can only assume it was full of white shirts, blue sport coats, and red ties since that's all I ever saw him wear.

He also allowed my grandmother and her sister sit in on rehearsal one afternoon after they toddled in from the casino to find me.

Years later, when Dick got sick and was bought out of the company, I had a run in with Dick Clark Productions, whose behavior wasn't as pleasant or ethical as their namesake. They are allegedly notorious for this type of behavior, an experience shared by many in the industry today.

The Late Show's Alan Kalter: I was at the holiday party thrown by my, then, commercial and voice over agency when I found myself in a corner with one of the agents and my friend, puppeteer extraordinaire, Tim Lagasse. Across the way, we noticed David Letterman's voice over man, Alan Kalter. Our agent called him over to say hello and as he walked towards us, Tim dared me to mess with Alan for a dollar. After we were all mutually introduced by first names and shook hands, the small talk began.

ME:
So have you been with the agency for a while?
ALAN:
Ya, about six years.
ME:
Oh nice. And what do you do?

He looks quizzical, surprised that I didn't know who he was.

ALAN:
Oh — um, I do voiceovers.
ME:
Really? Nice. How's that going? Are you booking?

He takes a beat, then gets that I'm screwing with him.

ALAN:
Gee it's going okay but do you have any suggestions?
ME:
Well what you need to do Alan — (hand on his shoulder)
... Alan is it? You see Alan ...

We all start giggling as Tim pulls out a dollar bill and hands it to me.

Alan was a warm, lovely guy, relaxed and fun. I reintroduced myself a few years later when I was booked for work at the Letterman show.

Lisa Lampanelli: Sweet, kinda shy, and very cute. We were on the bill together a few times and later I wrote jokes for the Roasts. I thought her persona was a lot funnier and more effective before she glammed up. Looking like a disheveled chick paralleled and supported her material.

'N Sync: I first met the guys when they did *Sesame Street*, where I got to lie between Justin Timberlake's legs with a puppet for quite some time. I remember I had my character drooling over him, spouting a long build up about how he has dreamed of meeting Justin for years to ask him one question...

"What's Britney Spears really like?"

I then reconnected with Joey Fatone a few years later when we worked on *Little Shop of Horrors*. He was so chill and easy going. I think having a baby made him pretty relaxed and ego-free. We'd hang at Club XL in New York with a group just getting our drink on.

Nelson Mandela: In 1994, I was working at a resort in the Bahamas. I was walking toward the main convention room to try and catch the last few minutes of the guest speaker when the doors opened up and the audience poured out. I was going against the tide of people twisting and dodging. I turned to come face to face with the special guest, Nelson Mandela. I was numb and probably had a blank stare on my face. He put his hand on my shoulder, said *hello*, and kept moving past.

Merv Griffin: I worked for Merv when he owned Resorts Hotel and Casino in Atlantic City. While not the producer, he was very hands-on with the Las Vegas-style production shows. I always felt bad for the singers and dancers because they were always in rehearsal due to changes from Merv.

He would walk in, toss a cassette to the producer and say, "I heard this song on the radio and I love it. Make it the new opening number." And of course, they would. He also decided that, once a month, he wanted to be in the show with a segment where he rolls out playing the piano doing some of his own act from the Coconut Grove.

The problem was, the music in these shows was tracked on reel-to-reel tape. So to keep changing the position of the production numbers meant they needed time to re-cut the show order, which there was rarely time for. They probably had eleven versions of the show. The sound engineer wanted to kill himself over and over.

Merv loved to hang with the cast. Especially the dancer boys and whatever new gorgeous male singer had been cast, whether they were straight or gay. There were a long list of crushes and in turn, considerations made for those he liked. Although he would often be seen at the hotel with Eva Gabor on his arm, in private he was usually hanging with Rip Taylor and each of their male arm candy.

Merv was super nice. But we were instructed that his parties were mandatory attendance ... part of the deal when working for him. As a comedy act, I think he could've cared less about me. I was young, new, not wearing a dance belt, and therefore not even in his peripheral vision.

I do recall when he decided to produce the next revue himself called, "S'Wonderful" based on the Gershwin song, he made us all listen to the new opening number where the chorus sang, "It's wonderful ... it's Merv-alous!" Pleased with the song, he buttoned it with his signature, "Oooooh-yesss."

Mike Myers: The endlessly talented, Canadian actor/puppeteer, Frank Meschkuleit invited Greg Ballora (*Team America & master builder*) and I to hang out and assist he and FX supervisor, Ron Stefaniuk on *The Love Guru*.

Pulling into the set we were told, "This has been a very tense set. Just know, it's not you. Mike has already had several people fired for staring at him." Mid-day, Greg found me behind a set piece waiting for Myers to leave the craft services table before I got myself a drink. I didn't want to take a chance of looking directly at him!

The great and difficult thing was that Myers would come up with gags he wanted to do on the spot, leaving Frank and Ron up all night or on another set figuring out how to do something before Mike finished a scene and asked for results. That makes for exciting creativity but a lot of anxiety. Having zero pressure on our part, Greg and I got to enjoy helping support them in their visions of engineering some of the bits, gags, special effects, and puppets.

While Mike was shooting one scene, we timed out the choreography to a fake set of legs that were to be strapped to him for a musical number. After spending quite a bit of time working it all out for the best and funniest effect, Ron shot it with a mini-cam and edited it on his laptop, erasing the puppeteers from the shot.

Mike walked in, saw it, then we sat quietly for ten minutes not looking directly at him (Like in *Raiders of the Lost Ark* where, if you looked in the wrong direction, your face melted off), while he *then* "came up with" the best way to do it ... which in the end was what we had already conceived ten minutes earlier.

I expected the Canadians to treat Mike like a king and they

did. After all, Canada only respects an artist once they leave Canada and make it in the States. But Hollywood may have taken its toll. Rumor had it Mike had a special umbrella person to follow him to his trailer, special sipping straw requests and special liquid temperature requirements.

Allegedly, the studio wouldn't let Mike direct the film so he hired the third assistant director from the *Austin Powers* movies as this director so he could boss the guy around and do whatever he wanted. But the pressure was on to do something good, so he was stressed. That, and apparently his wife issued him divorce papers on set as well.

I remember Verne Troyer (Mini Me from the *Austin Powers* movies) rolled in on his electric scooter to shoot his scene of the day. The director gave requests for Verne to say his one line "angry," then "sad," then "anxious" ... He delivered seven takes of the same line *identically*. "That's a rap for Verne everyone!" People applauded him and he scootered on his way. Job well done?

The movie was voted worst of the year. (Good thing *Gigli* had come out ten years prior...)

Wynonna Judd: I don't know why I was chosen to open for her. She was a good Christian lady and I was a loud Jew with an act full of innuendos.

I rarely saw her except when I'd leave the stage and she'd be entering.

ME:
Have a good show.
HER:
Thanks.

Finally, several shows later, I was vegging on a couch stage left with the singers and band when she plopped down next to me and said, "Hey little man."

I said, "A whole week and that's all I get?"

Hers was the first concert I performed where the room was so big they required huge jumbo screens on either side of the stage. No one's face should be magnified that big. It was horribly distracting and unforgiving. I'd only want a magnified face like that when I'm shaving...

Harrison Ford: Quiet, a guy's guy. He much preferred standing in a corner with men his age (custodians, accountants, anyone "normal") talking about horses, flying airplanes, and football teams. He was very soft spoken and attentive. He was not a star, he was an actor and allowed me to direct him. He just wanted to be told what to do and where to go.

William Shatner: I was in my late teens/early twenties and a stage tech at a dinner theater in a hotel, attached to a convention center, in Valley Forge, Pennsylvania. Yes — it was as random as it sounds. Forty minutes to show time we get a call from the GM. Shatner was on at a Sci-Fi convention next door, his sound system wasn't working and the natives (geeks) were getting restless. Could I and lead sound tech, Mark Kaplan, come right over?

Mark looked like Groucho Marx. He was a jittery guy and would make announcements on mic with all the wrong inflections to hilarious result. Example: When dedicating one performance to the sad passing of Robin Roe (pronounced "Row"), the daughter of our room manager, Mark announced it like someone had just won a new car. "Today's performance is dedicated to the memory of ROBIN ROOOOOOOE!" Completely inappropriate and yet wacky at the same time.

We get to the convention center and sure enough, there was William Shatner on a little platform stage in the middle of a sea of fans. There was a set piece that looked like a paper mache-like cave with fog and a glowing light coming from inside where Shatner would enter and exit. We arrived from the cave and joined him onstage. He said to us, "Oh, hello and thank God." As I was fiddling around with the wiring, I asked, "This is a circus. Is it always like this?" Wide eyed, he touched my elbow, "Oh you *don't* know." We got the mic up and running in a matter of minutes.

He wanted to give us a proper thank you but there were tons of people waiting for him to speak. So, like a proper tech, I just said, "There you go! Have a good time." exiting quickly to give him his stage as he publicly thanked the crew.

Barbra Streisand: Barbra Streisand was a part of numerous events I have worked on. If I recall correctly, Ms. Streisand's rider included flower petals in the toilet, needing to be "surrounded by beautiful things" which included countless bouquets of white roses, something about carpeting wherever she walked, and if any of the program was being televised, a very specific camera lens … a lens that they no longer make, but who's going to correct Barbra's overly-hyper team? Not me.

The lens effect they required was not dissimilar to the later years when Mary Hart had become a sort of glowing, golden hostess at the desk of *Entertainment Tonight*. We had to create an unfocused, golden hue on camera so basically Barbra was a fuzzy, golden Muppet with eyes and pearls.

Funny enough, she and Seth Rogen were on KTLA's morning show promoting the movie, *Guilt Trip*, when Seth outted her and her filtered camera on the air! Hilarious.

I will tell you one charming moment. After one show, I walked back into the dressing room thinking it was empty. She and her entourage were still prepping to leave. She looked older, a little tired, and it was clear her heels were causing discomfort.

She was surrounded by her "people." the group moved in unison toward the exit with her husband, James Brolin toddling behind. The herd stopped. The hand of the "Funny Girl" reached out from the crowd. He put his hand in hers as she pulled him into the center of the circle, holding his arm, they continued out the door. So charming. Really nice to see.

Oh — and she said "thank you" and "goodnight" to me as she went by.

Florence Henderson: Over the years I've had the privilege of opening for many "A" names. But my first time opening was a good enough way to begin.

I must have been around twenty-two. I got a call to drive to Atlantic City and open for Florence Henderson. I had only been sending videotapes out for a year or two. They must have been desperate and only read the fake bio info I wrote because the tape was awful. But this was an easy one-nighter. Two performances of fifteen minutes each.

I remember I was sitting in a dressing room all by myself just waiting. There was a small fruit tray and sodas. I was nervous and early. Not a great combo.

Finally at about ten minutes to show time, there was a knock at my door. And who leaned in but Florence Henderson. "Hi I'm Florence. You're allowed two *Brady Bunch* jokes and that's all." The door closed.

I wasn't even planning any *Brady Bunch* jokes! Was she used to hearing them? Was she saving the allotment for herself? So in a pinch, I told a joke suggesting Carol Brady had something to do with the demise of the first Mrs. Brady. I also, kind of, said she was "loose."

The joke went fine the first show. But the second show I told the joke and the audience was roaring. I just attributed it to me being more relaxed, until I turned around to see Florence standing over my shoulder with her arms crossed! She wagged her finger at me and left the stage.

A great sense of humor, she and her husband were terrific.

Jerry Lewis Telethon

Every act wanted to do the Jerry Lewis Telethon. Especially if Jerry was gonna be there during your slot. But the first time Eddie Foy Casting puts you on the air, you pay the dues of working the graveyard shift.

When I did it, the show was at the Sahara in Las Vegas. After 1:00 a.m., you're working to no one, so the sound engineer uses a laugh track. They really should have a live theatre engineer (not a studio guy) who knows proper timing!

Instead, my set went something like this:

I set up the joke.

I deliver the punch line.

Silence.

I start to set up the next joke.

LAUGH TRACK

... and so on ...

I wanted to murder that guy.

Phyllis Diller And Reno Throat

I was introduced to Phyllis Diller in Reno, Nevada. I entered her dressing room and she had a big smile. So cute and warm, she reminded me of my grandmother. Her show wig was on a foam headrest and as we were talking, she opened a shoebox and unwrapped these green, lacy, low-heeled shoes that matched her dress. As she pulled off the brown, almost butcher-like paper from the shoes, she told me these were the shoes she wore on the *Ed Sullivan Show*.

I'm thinking ... what? Who would keep shoes for so long? How did they last? The shoe company probably went out of business because they were so good, no one ever needed to buy new ones!

I had told her that when I first got to Reno, I had "Reno Throat." The climate dries your throat out so bad you sound like a frog. The hotel physician said it's very common for entertainers and he gave me a shot of Kenelog, a steroid. Phyllis asked, "Did you grow breasts?" I said, "I did and now I can sexually harass myself." She let out her signature cackle.

We were interrupted when a package came for her. It was from her daughter and it had been stinking up the mailroom all day. Turned out, it was cloves of garlic from her garden. She said it had kept her healthy for years.

Around 6:30 the next morning I got a call. It was Phyllis Diller instructing me to pick her up at her suite because we were going to breakfast. I didn't even know her but I guess she enjoyed my company.

The hotel butler opened the door and Phyllis toddled out in a tan raincoat with a little scarf around her head. She looked so tiny! She grabbed my arm and took me across the street to probably one of the last Woolworth's diners for the dollar-ninety-nine breakfast. I paid.

We talked all about comedy and family. But she didn't care to relive history. We talked about who she was today. She also shared her favorite quote, "Eat a spoonful of shit everyday so you remember the taste." She meant that there's always someone bigger than you to answer to and we all have to eat it once in a while.

I told her when I asked my little brother if he knew who Phyllis Diller was, he replied, "Sure. She was on Scooby Doo!" He was, of course, referring to a time in the '80s when Hanna-Barbara would animate special guest stars to make cameos in the cartoon. Phyllis threw her head back and clapped her hands, "Oh my gosh, that was so long ago! Funny!"

She gave me her number and invited me to come see her next time I was in Los Angeles. I did so about a year later. She lived in Brentwood right down the street from the O.J. Simpson house and crime scene.

Her house was very quaint and well designed. We went upstairs and she showed me two rooms full of rolled up carpeting and wallpaper. You could barely get inside. She collected them from garage sales, consignment shops and anywhere else. I knew she liked doing crafts but there was no way she was going to use two rooms full!

She shrugged and said she just liked to collect them. I don't think she was a hoarder. She just loved to find a great deal. Clearly frugal, this explained how she had kept that same pair of show shoes all those years!

Actor & New York Tour Guide,
Ron Silver

He always played the hard-ass, no nonsense, slick, smart, and many times quite a scary guy. He was also scandalously known for being a staunch, outspoken conservative in Hollywood. I used to confuse him with Andy Garcia. But after so many movies and television shows that included one of his last roles in *The West Wing*, I knew exactly who Ron Silver was when I got to work with him a year before his passing.

In league with people like Kevin Spacey, this guy was one of the finest examples of an actor I have ever had the honor of spending time with.

I was cast in my first movie and listed to co-star opposite huge names only because of my ventriloquism technique and having at least an ounce of acting capability with and without the puppet. I don't know that I was the best choice, but more likely, the least worst option.

On the third day of shooting, the car picked me up around 7:00 a.m. As we made our way up Manhattan's east side, I was informed we were making one more stop to pick up another actor. We pulled up to a high rise that was an old hotel turned Condo. But somehow they kept some of the hotel services going including room service and housekeeping! Posh.

Ron Silver casually and happily walked out of the building with his newspaper under his arm and hopped in the back seat. We were introduced, shook hands and started chatting about everything but work. This was a warm, gentle, calm, open, happy man.

He offered me the newspaper he had already read and

asked the driver if we could stop at a convenience store so he could pick up a *New York Times* and a coffee. We stopped, he asked me if he could get me anything, and ran into the store.

I looked down at the mailing label on his paper. It was addressed to "Mr. Leo Bloom." If you are not a theater buff, this was a character from the Mel Brooks film, turned Broadway musical, turned film remake, *The Producers*. Clearly, this was a pseudo name for his mail delivery to protect him from the general public. It is also a reference to one of my favorite shows. I felt like I had a guest pass to the inner circle. *So* show business!

As we continued to drive uptown to the location, Ron pointed out and gave detailed stories and personal anecdotes about the city's buildings, real estate, and history. I told him if the whole "acting thing" didn't work out, I could get him a gig with the Big Apple Bus Tours. He guffawed.

In this film, Ron played a big-time, Hollywood agent named Fielding Barnes who represented odd people and made them stars based on their physical shortcomings. I played his assistant, Harlan Swallow, who fulfilled his duties alongside Gary, a dummy sidekick, all perfectly natural to anyone in the office.

I was on set first, working on line delivery, puppet manipulation, and camera angles for the director and crew. Ron entered and watched me for a while, really interested as he took his place behind his desk.

He asked one or two questions about the shots. Then while everyone was chatting and doing final settings, I watched him look down at the desk, take a moment, and then raise his head to reveal his character, Fielding Barnes. I literally saw a transformation right in front of me. Intricate and subtle, I was now seeing the dickhead, egomaniac I've seen Ron Silver cast as so many times before, sitting right in front of me.

As I sat opposite him, he burrowed a stare right into my eyes. I realized he was engaging me in an acting exercise to filter everyone else out, feed each other energy, and build our character's dynamics. I respected him by setting aside any distractions or nervous energy to accept his unspoken offer as well as support him in his needs.

After a take or two, I had a question that was not heard by the director or DP. I got nervous or perhaps shy and decided to let it go and figure it out myself. I shot a glance over at Ron. He was watching me and spoke right up. "Go ahead, ask!"

I'm sure this cameo role wasn't a deep, difficult dig for him. But he was very focused throughout the work. After many takes and angles he was whisked away for some green screen shots and I stayed for a few pick-ups.

We were taken home separately so I never got to give him a proper goodbye, but I wrote to Mr. Leo Bloom the following week to thank him.

He passed away almost a year later from cancer of the esophagus. It was revealed he had been diagnosed two years earlier. He was sixty-two.

Control. Clarity. Focus. Kindness. Ron Silver. Pretty great.

I've Got You Under My Skin

There was a time in the early 2000's when Las Vegas not only went nuts producing Cirque shows, but for some reason Rat Pack tribute shows were popping up everywhere! It was vicious and the casting was never right for any of them.

Most guys just mimicked the icons of the group rather than doing genuine impersonations. Dean Martin wasn't too hard to cast ... tall, dark guy and a drinker. Sinatra was rarely depicted well. Young Franks, Old Franks ... most just did the voice and the mobster jokes but looked nothing like him, or resembled a shadow of him but didn't sound like him. But the Sammy Davis Jr.'s were always too tall or sounded more like a Muppet than anything else.

I get a call saying David Cassidy (The Partridge Family, EFX and DUIs) is desperately looking for a Sammy. Coincidentally I had just been working on the annual Broadway's Gypsy of the Year Benefit Show. This is a roster of sketches and musical numbers generally spoofing other shows, stars, producers and scandals of The Great White Way that season. I had just seen the cast of When Pigs Fly perform with a cameo appearance made by the late, Sammy Davis Jr. He was perfect: size, mannerisms, character and dialogue riffing and vocals. The house was screaming he was so good.

The man that played him was actor, Michael West (Forbidden Broadway and countless other credits). Michael was also white. I know what you're thinking but Michael wasn't doing blackface, he was doing a character!

I called Michael and asked him to send Cassidy a few clips and not to tell him his color. David loved him and a few days later as they started negotiating, I got a call.

DAVID CASSIDY:

Are you crazy??? I can't hire a while man to play Sammy Davis Jr.!

ME:

Why not?! He is amazing! And *you* didn't know!

DAVID CASSIDY:

The NAACP would go nuts. Forget it.

(click)

I called Michael and apologized. He knew it was a crapshoot. I think it would have been scandalous!!

Sundance:
Redford, Hopkins & Matis Yahu

I was asked to write a daily blog for the four to five days I attended Sundance for the movie, *The Ten* as a less affected newcomer. Here were some of the excerpts:

DAY 1:

What should I title the blog? My brother Kenny and I are in the hotel room now brainstorming and here's what we came up with:
- EXTRA CREDITS
- ACTOR SCHMACKTOR
- NAME DROPPINGS
- GRANDMA'S VAGINA (Ask Kenny)
- ERNEST GOES TO SUNDANCE
- WHERE IN THE HELL IS ROBERT REDFORD
- DO YOU KNOW WHO I AM?
& HOW MANY MORMONS DOES IT TAKE TO TURN ON A PROJECTOR?

I am an experienced traveler. Therefore I feel a little on edge with those who muck up the travel experience for me, like my new friend at Hertz Rent-a-car. I believe his name was, "Trainee."

Settled into the hotel and knowing that dining would be a nightmare, we Googled the local restaurants for reservations throughout the festival. After several listings of upscale establishments, I laughed my ass off at the most serious delivery of *this* information...

"...Low on cash? The 7-Eleven near the Park City Library has hot dogs, or better yet, skip the meal and stake a spot near the food table at a party."

Okay just to be clear, they are telling you to break in uninvited and steal food.

DAY 2:

Like everyone else, the day began just trying to see a film or two. It's near impossible. Sundance used to be about the little guy, his film vision and the people who support it. But now the corporate world has infiltrated and made it something else. I'll never forget Robert Redford opening the festivities with a speech that ended with a pan to the audience full of PR gurus and studio heads saying, "You guys fucked this whole thing up."

Main Street had a few companies hosting lounge socials and giving away samples of their products including one lounge promoting a healthy environment. I walked into the main room to find actor, Ed Begley Jr. riding a stationary bicycle to power up a stove or something! I thought maybe the elevation in Utah was finally kicking in and I was seeing things.

Tonight after a cocktail hour with tons of people I had never met, we went to the theater for the premiere.

To keep things in perspective, I walked to the red carpet's "step-and-repeat." The big names in the film walked in and flash bulbs went nuts. I walked in and everyone reloaded. Winona talked to *Entertainment Weekly* and I talked to *Animal Planet* by whom I'm asked to hold a goat.

It's hard for me to get that I was being included as one of the co-stars when they were moving me up to the tiny green room for a select few to be brought on stage prior to the film debut. It was myself, Adam Brody, Gretchen Moll, AD Miles, Paul Rudd, Ken Marino, Winona Ryder, Justin Theroux, and a few others. Winona and I reconnected and bonded instantly, along with Justin and me talking a lot about his own film premiering that week.

We were then joined by Famke Janssen, who is huge. My brother, in his Philly accent refers to as "FAMKEE JANSAN." With his repetitive mispronunciation of her name, I was confused and now believe that any one of the following versions could be correct in addressing her. They are ...

FAM-KEE JENSON
FAM-KAH JOHNSON
FOM-KAH JANSEN
FRANKA N'BEANS
FRAMPTON...
& SANKA

Before taking us into the theater with the public, David Wain walked in to explain about the introductions and the Q&A after, but not before he told everyone how touched he was that we came to support him at this huge life moment. It was really nice. He's so sweet.

During the Q&A, someone actually asked, "Who performed the ventriloquist dummy?" David praised me and my work very generously.

DAY 3:

After a day of chillin' with the boys (Rudd, Wain, LoTruglio) and watching the game at their rented house, we all headed over to the *Premiere Magazine* party for our film. It was the most anticipated party and security was tight. But after walking the carpet and chatting it up with everyone, we moved to a private lounge overseeing the entire party where, after all was said and done, we just played!

Music by New York's spinmaster, Mr. Blue, walk-in friends of the cast, like SNL's Rachel Dratch and film actor, Sam Rockwell. But the highlight of the evening was a surprise appearance and performance by orthodox, reggae rapper, Matis Yahu, whose concert was sold out Friday night and was now here rocking the friggin' house.

The talk is *The Ten* has several studios bidding for it now.

I have never seen a cast *and* crew care so much for a project to come and support! This was all amazing.

Playing Las Vegas

Every act wants to play Vegas in their career. I was so lucky to work the strip before Cirque and the big magic shows pummeled the booking market for any other variety act that once made the town famous.

But in the late '80s and '90s there were still big revue shows like *Enter the Night* or *Jubilee!* — the show your grandparents saw on their honeymoon. There were comedy headliners at Caesar's Palace and the most fantastic camp shows like *Boylesque* and *Bottoms Up!* on the marquees.

Unknown names were huge stars in the middle of the desert. Bobby Berosini and his orangutans, The Great Tomsoni and Company, or in recent years someone like the late Danny Gans.

In Danny's case, The Rio Hotel & Casino needed a performer to compete with the neighboring Siegfried & Roy show amongst others. They plucked the unknown, pretty average impressionist and repackaged him, launching a huge PR campaign and created a star in this microcosm called Las Vegas.

It was 1997 and I was working in Biloxi, Mississippi at the Grand Theatre, a brand new 2000-seat facility when the power went out mid-show. Always thriving during emergencies, I went out to fill time until the crew could reboot the system.

I grabbed a candle from one of the tables, felt my way back to the stage, and yelled out to the audience, "Can everyone see the floating candle?" I then proceeded to do eight minutes in the dark.

It went great. Well enough that Dick Feeney, producer of *Viva Las Vegas* at the Stratosphere and *The Flying Elvi* came backstage and said, "If you can do that well off-the-cuff and in the dark, you should come do my show in the light."

Viva Las Vegas was a long running, little afternoon show that every local Las Vegas act wanted to do. Not because the show was that good or the money was big but because it was a regular day gig that allowed you to stay in town and also book a night gig too.

If I recall the timeline correctly, I was simultaneously working on getting into *Folies Bergere* at the Tropicana. I got a call on a Thursday offering me the *Folies* job. Friday I was told they were giving the job to the aforementioned Bobby Berosini.

Berosini was a huge comedy act in the 1970s and '80s with trained orangutans (seen in Clint Eastwood's *Every Which Way But Loose*) until PETA got a hold of security video of him beating the animals. He was run out of town and ended up years later in Branson, Missouri, doing a show with, like, one monkey (or a squirrel dressed up like a monkey).

As luck would have it, PETA got wind of his possible return and threatened to picket the hotel if he was hired. Thus, I was offered eight shows a week at $3500. Which, for a young act, was amazing, plus I was doing the *Viva* show by day.

When I first played Las Vegas, I was young and I lived the role. It was like playing dress-up with flashy clothes, dabbling in donning a ring or two and I wore sunglasses in doors. Now I look at those guys and think ... what a douchebag. But *so* fun at the time.

Over the next fifteen years I played Las Vegas many times at clubs like The Riviera or Comedy Stop, opening for star names like Kenny Rogers or Tom Jones, or as a comedy headliner in the big production shows like *Skin Tight* or *Splash*. Performing there was a lot of fun. Living there is something else...little culture and lots of crime, irregular boobs and regular inbreeding.

The Famed Beverly Hilton Hotel

In 2009 I moved to L.A. to see if I could break out of the corner career I had painted myself into. Then the economy tanked and so did my work. I was also in a relationship with someone who fell on harder times than me. Things were bad. The 99 Cent Store was the only place I shopped for months. So to make ends barely meet, I went back to where I began, as a tech.

Long time friend and super woman, Rachel Wolfe was the boss of a stage tech company and gave me hours on whatever jobs she had at the famed Beverly Hilton Hotel. (The Jewish clientele of Bev Hills would fawn over Rachel until they realized it was Rachel Wolf with an E, not Jewish, followed by a below-zero, about-face in warmth and interest.)

I was working double time, flying home from a gig performing somewhere around the world, getting into my tech blacks to go push anvils, unload trucks and tear down shows all night long.

Eventually I'd move up the food chain. Spotlight job here, running camera there. I'd get a call, "Hey can you run a jib cam? It's $300 more than on sticks." I mean, in theory I knew how to do it. I'd seen it done enough times. Just don't bang anyone in the head with it and you're golden.

It was the set up and trouble-shooting of the equipment that I had no idea about. I hadn't tech'd equipment for fifteen years. So when the TD would say, "Ziggy can you make sure the Z5200 is in the rack?" I'd take a beat, use the power of deduction and reply, "Oh, the big, black thing with all the cords coming out of it? Sure." Then I'd go stare at the rack for five minutes until I had the balls to quietly ask someone what to do.

It was KYW and Janet King all over again. Thank God for kind engineers that took pity on me (on both coasts...).

Eventually I got calls and referrals for the most high profile events. Hand held camera wasn't the most prestigious but was a favorite of mine. I hung off the ropes shooting *Celebrity Boxing* with fists just millimeters from my head, concerts with security holding crowds off my back as my images went live, and as mentioned earlier, I was called as the exclusive cam op for Will and Kate at a Technology Summit. It was their first stop in the US after the wedding.

I was eventually brought in as stage manager, tech director, production manager/supervisor, or show director for events with the old and new famous: Morgan Freeman, Barbra Streisand, Harrison Ford, Whitney Houston, Kirk Douglas, Buzz Aldrin, Ziggy Marley, Wanda Sykes, Mickey Rooney, President Barack Obama, and of course it was the hotel where Whitney Houston died; a story and details of which I am privy to. I was asked to share it with entertainment news shows and for this book but I chose not to.

The tough part, working as a tech again, was being in the same room with the people I had co-starred with in the past, opened for, or dreamt of working with. "Hey, Mel Brooks! Great to see you...Who me? Oh — I'm here with, for...on camera two. Enjoy the chicken." But I was grateful. Without the day job and the friend who gave it to me, I'd have never made it through.

I have always loved tech and have always kept a set of black clothes and a bag of tools in the closet. Understanding tech as well as performance allowed me to be a strong designer and director for my shows along with my clients over the last fifteen years.

Like many historic properties, the Beverly Hilton has to charge a ton of money to clients when, in fact, it is ... to be kind, not up to the standards one might expect.

In fairness, when the late Merv Griffin — who I worked for in AC years before — (See: Merv Griffin) sold the hotel to the current owner, he sold a property that was in desperate need of an aesthetic and structural facelift. (He also left his collection of parrots, the last of which are still positioned and tended to in a hallway off the lobby.)

What Merv did not mention was that the historical society would not allow the owners to alter the structure in any way, leaving them with a dated, aging, expensive hotel battling for competitive facilities.

This also made it a huge and grueling undertaking for the house production team to facilitate full load ins, set and strikes, rehearsals, unions, labor, fire marshals, press and security when there is a different show at least every other day.

By the way, these technicians had amazing show business careers of their own. One of my favorite friends and most difficult of the techs was "BG" He was a big, bald, gruff guy who was also sweet and funny and everyone's buddy ... except the clients, which was what generally created the problem.

As a sound engineer for numerous rock and roll icons and more recently, *Wheel of Fortune* and *Ellen*, he loved music and he loved sound. As far as he was concerned, it was the most important thing in a show. "No audience ever goes home humming the lights," he'd say.

"BG" passed away a few weeks ago from a heart attack. It was so perfect that the very opening of the service had microphone feedback! I know where ever he was, he was throwing his hands up in the air having a fit.

I worked on numerous events and productions in the hotel's International Ballroom, home of the Golden Globes, Oscar & Grammy luncheons, concerts, the *People's Choice Awards*, royal, presidential, and political summits and every major charity event there was.

It was jaw-dropping the way every celeb you could think of would whore themselves out to participate in events at this historic hotel just to be seen, and rub elbows with the rich.

But not all of my moments there were my finest. Like when I dropped a handheld camera during a live award show in front of a table of Hollywood heavyweights including Annette Benning and Warren Beatty.

I had no wrangler that night and the cable got caught, pulling the camera out of my hands. The stars gasped as it crashed to the floor. The presenters continued on stage and I knelt down, to not attract more attention, when Zach Galifanakis leaned down to me and giggled, "Just stand right up and start handing out business cards."

The Pointer Sisters
Make Fun Of My Virginity

My family loved The Pointer Sisters. So much so that, when I had my first serious girlfriend, my mother sat me down and told me to listen to the song, "Slow Hand." She said the lyrics would guide me on how to treat the girl during intimacy. Yes, I'm serious.

In the early '90s I wanted to step into the opening act booking scene but I didn't know how to begin. Remember, it was before the Internet, so getting jobs really took hustling ... four-one-one, the yellow pages, and the local papers.

I was performing at a casino where The Pointer Sisters would be appearing in a few weeks. I thought, what could be more convenient? I was already there.

I went to the record store, flipped over a Pointer Sisters album, found the record company, called the company's PR office, got the act's agency representation, called them, got the management company, called them. I then pleaded my case. They agreed to consider it but would have to get the okay from the William Morris Agency.

A little overzealous, I called the WMA to help things along, only to be called by the management, cursed out for overstepping my bounds, followed by *"You'll never open for anyone ever in this town!"* an expletive, and a crashing down of the phone receiver.

However weeks later was my first of numerous openings for the sisters.

They sounded amazing every night, as good as the recordings. Aside from the more well known songs like "I'm So

Excited," "Neutron Dance," and "Jump For My Love." I had no idea how many other countless songs they wrote for singers and movie soundtracks, a very impressive songbook.

They traveled to each job separately. Separate flights and car services, separate contract riders. Let's just say there was tension, although not as bad as Hall & Oates, who won't even enter from the same side of the stage.

One sister required seventeen shrimp in her shrimp cocktail. No more, no less. All celebrities ask for crazy shit. Barbra Streisand's flower petals in the toilet, Sheena Easton's carpet de-germing, Steve & Edie's special European ketchup for steak they wouldn't swallow, only chew up for the juice then spit out on the plate.

But the sisters were very kind. Ruth Pointer was the nicest to me. At one point in my working with them, she found out about my mother's "Slow Hand" sex talk story. The stage manager called me from my dressing room. The sisters were calling me to come on stage. They sat me on a stool and sang "Slow Hand" while mocking my virginity as a young man! The audience loved it. I was embarrassed and flattered at the same time.

My Worst Night
& The Millionaire That Went To Prison

Oh yes. Karma and I know each other very well. As I've mentioned, there was a long time in my career that I would try to micromanage the universe. I would get an amazing opportunity based on my good name, then I would do something to try to move it along faster, and Karma would pay me a visit, shooting myself in the foot and looking like an asshole. It took me years to learn that lesson. But Lady K has also taken care of me by balancing things out when I have been wronged. This brings us to the worst day of my professional life.

It was around 1996 and I was the comedy guest star in a production show where I met singer who we'll call Dana Jones, a blond, Alabama, southern belle type. I think she referred to her father as "Big Daddy" and everyone used their first and middle names. William Scott, Bobby Ray ... you get the idea.

It's strange Dana and I became friends. I was a loud, Jewish, gay guy and she was a refined, Christian, southern girl. Although, get to know her and she can dish it out like the devil and nobody's business ... *"bless her heart."* (That's what southerners say after ripping someone to shreds.) I enjoyed her.

I was raised to hold the door open for a lady. And Dana was raised to let a man do it or it would be unladylike. One day we got to a door, stopped and I didn't reach for it. We stood there for a few seconds until she giggled and said, "What are you doin?" I replied, "What? Are your arms broken? Open the door!"

Dana was also taught that a lady doesn't go out without full hair and makeup. When I called her up the first time and told her to throw something on and let's go see a movie, "throwing on something" took two hours. You gotta love her.

We had just met and were rehearsing for the show. During the rehearsal, Dana approached me. "Hi. It's Zieg-*feld*, right?

"Yes," I replied. "Like the Follies."

The overture finishes and the opening number begins. I hear Dana in the corner trying to burn my name into her brain. "Feld. Feld. Feld."

She is cued for my voiceover introduction.

"Ladies and gentlemen, Mr. Michael *Feld*-man!"

That was a new one. I've gotten Ziegfield, Ziegler, Zigfled, Zigzeld, Figfeld, Zigfiled, and Seinfeld, but Feldman was now at the top of my list. She was embarrassed. It was cute. Because of errors like that and for other reasons, I now go by "Michael Paul" in most of my work.

I know what you're thinking. What does any of this have to do with Karma and the "worst day of my professional life?" I'm getting to that.

Dana and I worked together again two years later. Following one performance, I was introduced to her best girlfriend and her husband, a man named Richard Scrushy. They had thick southern accents just like Dana. Richard was over the moon for my act. He explained that he owned a healthcare company and every year they did a huge national corporate meeting for the employees and stockholders. In between the weekend of meetings, speeches and awards they brought in star entertainment. Richard wanted to hire me and he gave me his card.

Dana later told me that he was in every Fortune 500 magazine for business, *Better Home & Gardens*, and every other aspect of the couple's personal and professional life. Some other points of interest were: Richard was also a wanna-be musician and paid name performers to be in his band. He had a museum dedicated to himself in the lobby of his corporate office and he was paying for Dana to have studio time at Sony Country Music with access to the Sony Library. Lastly, I realized Richard's company, HealthSouth, had been employing my mother in Philadelphia for a few years now. Weird.

I had performed many corporate events in the past. I knew how to do them. It's a very different bird especially if you are not a household name where they *know* what they are going to get. Although, a synagogue hired Joan Rivers and they were offended by how filthy she was. HELLO? You hired Joan Rivers!

But when you are playing to a bunch of suits, it can be touchy. They generally do not want to let loose in front of their boss. Also, some bosses don't want to be teased. It's generally a good idea to do your homework on the company, i.e. what they do, where they came from, who their competitors are, and any of the more personal, inner office "water cooler" talk.

The other issue for a performer's success or failure is placement of the entertainment within the evening. Everyone thinks the entertainment is the "big finish" and should go at the end. That is dead wrong. So not to go on a long, boring harangue, let me break the format down in a few key bullet points. Maybe you'll have a better appreciation for the performer:

Room set up is important. Once I was told there was going to be a stage for me. They did not tell me it was separated from the audience by what seemed like a two mile long dance floor. People are morons.

The Act should go on *after* dinner, dessert, coffee, and the dishes are cleared away. People have ADD. You can never compete with food because people are animals, and waiters with clinking glassware are easy distractors.

The Act goes on *before* awards and speeches. Why?

Once people get their award, they want to get home and pay (celebrate with) the baby sitter.

After a whole evening the people are tired of sitting, they are drunk or have food coma. No way can they deal with another forty-five minutes no matter how big your name is or how good you are.

Chances are, the VPs or department heads will have prepared a skit or slide show that bombs and goes on way too long, thereby making the Act's job harder to bring everyone back to the "land of awake."

It never fails. Someone will make a speech that is so

depressing or awkward, there is no recovery.

"D" is the worst and the nightmare of most performers. Every time I let the client force me into submission to do it their way, it was a train wreck.

Example: There was a period when this booker would keep calling to bring me in for Orthodox Jewish groups. When I told him, "Thank you but I'm not the act for you," he insisted these were hip, contemporary people (that can't be touched, don't like Jewish jokes, let their kids run around, and will not laugh out loud).

These shows would never go well and then I'd get another call, "They loved you and want you back!" offering me more money to return.

The final booking was an event that insisted on giving out the big award before my act. I told them I wouldn't be responsible for how the rest of the evening went.

Sure enough, the man took the award and then spoke about the Holocaust for thirty minutes. BRING ON THE COMEDY! The Holocaust? Why don't we tack on abortion and slavery to round out the royal ass-fucking before I go on?

SIDEBAR: AS I WRITE THIS PART OF THE STORY, I'M ON A PLANE. AN ANNOUNCEMENT WAS JUST MADE LOOKING FOR A NURSE OR DOCTOR. NO ONE EVER CALLS FOR A COMEDIAN OR VENTRILOQUIST. I GUESS I SHOULD BE HAPPY. I'M SURE I'D JUST PULL FOCUS FROM THE PATIENT. — *"Sure you're dying, but what about me!"*

I had learned a while back that you don't take every job just because you'll get paid to do comedy. If it's not your audience, you'll end up failing, rejected and pissing people off. Remembering what Rickles told me: "Find your audience."

It's very similar to why young actors feel so rejected. They audition for roles just because it's their gender or eye color. Just audition for your type! Even if it means you are going out on fewer auditions.

The next week I called Richard Scrushy at HealthSouth headquarters. I told him that the show he and his wife enjoyed in the privacy of a casino show as a couple, might not be the right fit for a southern, corporate health care company. He wouldn't take *no* for an answer and told me to name my price, and then transferred me over to my new point man, his company vice president.

I not only continued to express my concerns but, over the next few months, I sent them tons of material to review. I was assured they had seen it and it was all fine. So I named my price, sent the contracts, and it was all set. I'd be performing at the Dolphin Resort in Disney World for five thousand people.

Two months later, my mother got laid off. Out of the blue, my phone rings.

"Michael? Richard Scrushy here. Listen I just heard about your mother getting laid off and I'm embarrassed about it. I just wanted to assure you that I am handling this personally and your momma has nothing to worry about." *Click.*

That week my mother was brought back to work. It's not the same position exactly. In fact, she wasn't really doing much at all. It was clear that, once my performance ended, so would her temporary gravy train.

Two months later, my assistant Sharon and I flew first class to Florida. (I don't usually have an assistant. I just didn't wanna go alone and the money was right!) We got to the convention space — a multi-media event spectacular three ballrooms long with lighting grids, IMAG screens, multiple cameras on dollies, sticks, and jibs.

Richard's wife approached me, as she was in charge of the evening. She welcomed me, gave me the rundown of the schedule, then inquired what material I'd be doing. I told her I'd be doing the material she saw at the casino. Her eyes got wide and she said, "You can't do that."

My gut hurt. Attempting to keep my composure, I asked: "Well, why are we discussing this two hours before I go on? I sent tons of material for approval over the last six months!"

Richard walked in with security and his VPs. I walked through his security, stood in front of him and said flat out, "You do realize what I'm going to be doing tonight, right?" He assured me he did and it would be great. I didn't believe it. I knew I was in trouble but I did everything I could do to cover my ass. Or so I thought.

Numerous sports figures were in attendance, clearly as eye candy for the awards ceremony and I was told I'd be opening tonight for singer, Amy Grant. I knew nothing about Amy but I found out later that she went from a Bible thumper to mainstream country music.

Up to this point, the HealthSouth conventions only booked musical acts. They had never used any type of act with theatrical cues. So, when they were running late in rehearsals because the wife cared more about what table the awards would sit on, my rehearsal was cut. This breach of contract created a larger problem later on. But I prepped the sound engineer and went to chill, eat, and shower.

When Sharon and I got backstage, we were told the evening was running late and I was asked to cut eight to ten minutes. No problem.

I entered the stage and began the set. It was a sea of people but I could only see pitch darkness with the exception of the first three rows. Richard and company were front row, center.

About ten minutes in, I saw that Richard was uneasy. I wasn't bombing by any means. However with all the technology purchased for the evening, they had neglected to include a sound system to counter the delay of my microphone. The result was the audience sitting three convention rooms deep would hear my joke and respond one section at a time. There wasn't one, big, group laugh at any one time, so to an untrained ear, it may have seemed like things weren't going well.

At this moment Amy Grant had told the stage manager that the evening was running too long and she wanted to go on *now*. Generally when they want to cue a performer to get off, they blink a light or stand in the wing and give a "wrap it up" signal. In the worse case, they find a break in the act that sounds like a last joke and play the act off with some music and an announcement. However, these people had never dealt with a verbal act before. If my contracted rehearsal had been honored, they would have known I was finishing up anyway. Instead, they chose to simply stop playing my cues.

As an experienced performer, I assumed there was a technical problem so I started to stretch. They wanted me off and I was going longer. Every few minutes I'd ask the techs, "How we doin?" Nothing. No one talked to me. After five to eight minutes I was in a panic. I ran out of material, the room was quiet, and there was no way to end the set fluidly... that is, if they were even ready backstage! How could I know? They left me out to dry. Finally, I started telling the only joke that popped into my head, an old stock joke about a priest and a nun.

Two lines in, Richard Scrushy came bounding up on stage with a microphone cutting me off. "Okay that's enough of that!" He put me in a headlock and turned our backs to the audience with a look of fire in his eyes, pushing me off stage. I played it off like a *"get outta here ya crazy kid"* type of thing.

Before I could hit the wing, he began an evangelical tirade against me. He called me trash. "HealthSouth doesn't condone that kind of smut!" He went on for eight minutes.

The crew was pissed. I was freaked. Sharon and I grabbed our shit and ran to the hotel room.

A few things were going through my mind. The guilt by association via Dana and my mother's embarrassment, the rest of my money that was owed following the performance, and the out-of- body loathing and humiliation I had just experienced in front of 5000 people.

I called Dana. I knew she blamed me, thinking I had just been irresponsible. She was shocked and speechless. My mother was very upset and begged me to let it go, knowing I was still owed money. "But Michael," she said. "They have deep pockets and big lawyers!" I told her I was an equal when we negotiated and I'm an equal now.

The next morning we were walking past members of the convention audience as we checked out. Some were also on our flight home. The stares were painful.

Funny though ... some people were unaffected, asking if that was a part of the show. Others liked me and thought Scrushy was an ass. The rest smirked and muttered names at me.

I was numb as I walked into my apartment. The first thing I did was sit down at my desk and start writing the letter to the HealthSouth executive team. Three and a half pages outlining the six months of careful participation leading up to this event, the serious breaches of contract, and numerous acts disregarding our agreement that would have prevented this occurrence. Not to mention the fact that Richard Scrushy put his hands on me. I concluded by telling them I expected the balance of my fee to be overnighted and received by five o'clock tomorrow. I faxed it.

My mom begged me to leave it alone. But the next day I received a FedEx with my check and a simple note that stated, "We disagree with your assessment." Well, what else *could* they say??

Weirdly enough, the next night I had a small, local 500-seat corporate booked. I actually had a great show. But my mother was let go from the company and Dana's studio time ended.

For the next three years I was a mess. Gun-shy. I lost my confidence. Every time I'd hear a southern drawl or when a client would ask about my material I'd get IBS and be in the bathroom until show time.

Not long after that event, Richard Scrushy joined the ranks of Enron and other corporate executives when he was brought up on federal charges for fraud, money laundering, obstruction of justice, racketeering, and bribery. (If I had a voice I'd add piss poor party planning, but it looked like he was already in enough trouble...) The FBI sting turned many of his HealthSouth vice presidents against him. He served time. I love you, *Karma*.

You'll be happy to know that, with time and experience I regained my confidence. Dana and I stayed friends, even after another unfortunate mishap when I suggested a quaint restaurant for her and a Sony Country Music exec's NYC brunch. The new spot was adorned with local artists' paintings. The week I was there, it was flowers and butterflies. I had no idea they changed out the artwork weekly. The day Dana and company went, it was black and white photos of gay, male erotica. Fuck.

(I ate there three times later that week...)

Howdy Doody Ruined My Life

One night my parents were entertaining me and, to keep me busy, they sat me down for the premiere of *The All New Howdy Doody Show*. It was 1976 and the producers of the original *Howdy Doody Show* decided to bring it back in living color ... or "livid color" as Mr. Doody told me when we met years later. My mom made me a bowl of popcorn (made fresh in a pot on the stove, no microwave popcorn yet), and then I saw it. The red and white striped puppet stage, the blue curtain, Buffalo Bob, the Peanut Gallery and then, something I had never seen before.

He was a little wooden man with freckles, a cowboy outfit and a big grin. I saw the strings but it didn't ruin the moment. In fact, it enhanced it. On the surface I was bubbling with excitement over a puppet. But subliminally I was enthralled knowing there were people hidden away controlling him. How? Where? I began my deep love for puppetry and the hidden technical side of show business.

My parents used to scold me for spending too much time in front of the television. But I wasn't just turning my brain to mush watching the "idiot box" as mom called it. I'd notice the shadow of the boom mic on *The Cosby Show*. I'd wonder how they shot the last camera angle on a fourth wall when I knew the set only had three on *Cheers*. And I'd catch the head of Muppet creator Jim Henson accidentally poke into camera shot when performing the most famous frog.

Howdy Doody sparked my greatest love for a lifetime, puppeteering. As I mentioned, years later I was producing a television pilot pitch and needed a special guest. I had befriended the puppet master that had been tapped by Bob

Smith to refurbish Howdy (his friends call him that) for special appearances. Later he would take over performing the iconic character when he would leave his post at the Smithsonian. With proper legal guidelines in order, the powers that be agreed to bring Mr. Doody (everyone else calls him *that*) to the set.

It was a very young audience and crew. But when the host's interview was wrapped, even the coolest of the cool were standing in line to snap a photo with Howdy Doody.

In between takes, we kept the cameras rolling and Howdy and I did a little bit together. It connected my childhood to adulthood. Once watching him on TV and now directing him, it was one of my happiest days.

Two years after the premiere of *The All New Howdy Doody Show*, it was cancelled. My mother and I sat down to write a letter to the studio in New York City. I received a reply on Doodyville stationary talking about ratings and such, thanking us for our support and viewership. From that point on, all I wanted were puppets. I had bags and bags of them. I'd rip them apart and glue others together to make new characters.

In second grade my parents bought me a portable, transformable puppet stage for hand puppet and marionette shows. Mrs. Green, the secretary of my elementary school, gave me a piece of mimeograph paper. I loved the smell of the ink. Didn't you? I made a hand-written flyer (I was a lefty so there was ink smearing of course) for puppet shows. Twenty dollars for one show; twenty-five for both.

Scouts, schools and birthday parties were my clientele. The shows consisted of bits, lip-syncing, and handing out party favors. My mother was my production manager, driving me around and engineering the record player. She never took a cut.

Eventually the puppets were set aside because my grades were slipping as I became less interested in school. Nor would puppets help a young man's social life.

But like many, I was obsessed with *Sesame Street* and later, the Muppets and anything Jim Henson. Even back in elementary school it weighed heavily on me that by the time I would/could grow up and get to New York to work for the

Muppets, *Sesame Street* might be off the air! (The birth of my Jewish neurosis.)

Since then I have puppeteered for commercials, movies, television, and trained the casts of *Avenue Q* and Disney's *The Lion King*. (I think I could have been in the first casts of *Lion King* but Julie Taymor felt that anyone with Jim Henson on their resume should not be seen for auditions. "That kind of puppeteering was commercial, not artistic.")

I love puppetering most of all. If there was enough work, I'd be happy to give up everything else.

James Brown Takes Us To The Movies

It was the last show of the week at a casino. My show would be "dark" the next day because James Brown would be appearing. There was no way the cast wasn't going to see "The Godfather of Soul." We were brought back stage and ushered into the dressing room where James's manager, nicknamed "The Judge" pulled me aside and asked, "You were the ventriloquist from last night's show right? The Godfather would like you to send us your materials to perhaps open for him."

On cue, the bathroom door swings open. Leather from head to toe, petrified hair and huge white, Chicklet teeth, the five foot nothing icon says, "At's right! We bin lookin for a ventrikolist fo' da sho!"

Those were the last words I ever understood that came from his mouth. Thank God, I became friends with his "black-up singers." Mr. Brown would say something to me. He'd walk into the other room. I'd look at the girls questioningly and they'd whisper, "Go get paid!"

One of the fascinating things about James was that his entourage was just the boys from the old neighborhood: huge black men in velvet suits with lots of jewelry. When James wasn't walking around with a wad of 100s to tuck into shirt pockets, his boys would do it for him, asking people to "handle that problem for Mr. Brown." It was very old-school show business.

James was very generous. He took us all to the movies when we were in Georgia. It was a predominately black audience. In his neighborhood, *Schindler's List* played for a weekend, but *Sister Act 18* would be there for ten months.

Mid-movie, one of the girls wanted me to re-enact an embarrassing moment my mother once had in a theater. It involved her feeding me a black licorice, Juicy Fruit candy, knowing I didn't care for them. I spit it out yelling, "*Ugh*! *I* hate *the blacks*!" Sixty eyes turned to stare at me when James Brown leaned over and says, "You on yo' own!"

I was the only white guy on the tour or in the theaters we played for most shows. My first night performing I was just okay. I could feel that I was in "their house." I had to show I acknowledged that. So the second night I dressed a little looser and started out with improv with the audience before pulling out the puppets. I played it *super* white. They knew I was making fun of myself *and* the situation. They gave me the okay, and I killed.

When there were breaks in the tours, the return dates were iffy due to James's legal problems, so you had to be flexible to work the tour. I told The Judge, if they'd just book us in prisons and narcotic clinics we'd never be out of work!

James was truly the hardest working man in show business. When I worked with him he was around sixty-nine and still doing the splits that made him famous. Many older singers are on stage for forty minutes or so. Then they give a song to the band, the backup singers, they use video clips and fillers like that. James did two-hour shows where he never left the stage. R-E-S-P-E-C-T.

The shows were also super-casual. Random people (I assume they were friends) would just wander onto and across the stage in the middle of a number to talk to a band member, pour a drink, or look for their car keys.

The first time I saw James work, I awaited for the historical moment in his performance when he kneels down on one knee, head to his chest. He simply cannot go on, when a man walks out and covers him in the most lavish cape to console him before he snaps to attention, throws off the cape and brings the song home.

When the moment came, it definitely wasn't what I was expecting. An old black man came hobbling out on stage in a pinstripe, three-piece suit with a duffle bag. He pulled out the cape, dropped it over The Godfather's shoulders, and before

James could possibly feel consoled, pulled it off, crumpled it up, stuffed it back in the bag, threw it over his shoulder and meandered off stage. *So* anti-climactic!

It turns out, the young boy James threw a coin to fifty years ago to be his consoling cape keeper was that same man still doing it to this day, now hobbling out on stage as he had done hundreds of times before, probably in between watching his TV shows in the dressing room.

When James died, I was honored to be invited to the viewing at The Apollo. Only months earlier I had worked with the famous theater on a tribute to Phyllis Hyman. The only show ever approved by her family. (Phyllis was a young, sultry voiced singer who was taking R&B by storm until she committed suicide before a performance at The Apollo.)

The Pointer Sisters, The Mills Brothers, James Brown, The Apollo ... white boy got some game.

How A Magician's Lion
Helps You Win A Car

I was once asked to consult for a producer who's product I never cared for. Her delusions of self-importance were absurd. Don't misunderstand. Every producer I've ever met thinks they are Spielberg or Andrew Lloyd Webber.

I once sat in the audience of the Las Vegas cirque show, *O*, next to a cabaret lounge producer whose show's popularity was due to the hotel's papering (free tickets). He ripped the multi-million dollar, world renowned, super spectacular to shreds! I turned to him in all my New York-ness and said, "Ummmm...your show is a sign, a curtain and eight karaoke tracks!"

Back to the story....

The producer for this job was originally a dancer. Producers who come from one area of the business produce shows that are heavily based in the one aspect they know about while the alternate, equally important layers are lacking or missing (Lights, dialogue, music, transitions, arc ... beginning, middle, endings!).

Her sets and costumes may at times have been expensive, but were usually generic designs, very abstract or just built for look, not longevity. She'd spend a few thousand dollars on Armani suits for a singer she loved, but wouldn't pay for dancers' costume cleanings for six months at a time. Her male dancers were sometimes so fem, you didn't know who was supposed to be leading and the female dancers notoriously stuck their fingers down their throats just to please her.

The current show she was producing was a magic show and

the stars of it were a sort of, "Siegfried & Roy" *light*. These guys had one cat in the act (I think it was a panther) that was old and had maybe one tooth. At night, the cat probably kept that tooth in a glass by his bed... The producer built the show around them and decided she was going to rent them a lion. I'm not sure where you do that. Amazon? Lions-R-Us? Is there a zoo with a lease-to-buy plan or layaway? Even if you know nothing about show business, clearly this is a bad idea. Even your dog needs to bond with you before handling them, right?

The producer was notorious for her mood swings and was in a particularly bitchy mood during this set-in (mounting a new show), cracking the whip and talking to people like trash. But karma would soon pay her a visit.

Her company sent invitations and flew in hotel and casino entertainment directors from around the country for opening night to woo them into contracting her for their properties.

8:00 p.m. The front rows are made up of entertainment directors and the casino high-rollers. The curtain goes up, the opening number climaxes, the lion appears, and the place goes wild!

The magicians walk the beast down the ramp to the VIP booths when the animal stops, lifts its leg, and pisses on the whole front row. The thick yellow stream hits a table and sprays out. Stinky-lion-pee. I could smell it all the way up in the tech booth. People were not pleased. It was *awesome*.

After the show I heard the man who got the largest of the golden shower also won a car in the casino. Coincidence, my ass.

Thank you, Karma. Nice to see you again.

On... Off...Well, Next to Broadway

I have always regretted never having gone to a performing arts school in my youth. 'Till the day I die I will always wonder and be envious of those that can express themselves through song and dance, in addition to the rare few that also have real acting chops to back it all up

Perhaps I didn't have the skills, opportunity or maybe I just didn't have the balls to relax, let go and give in.

I have decided to bypass the story of my 18 year old, uneducated, untrained attempt to audition for Broadway's revival of "Damn Yankees" complete with wardrobe and a faulty flashpot entrance. Mortifying ignorance is bliss.

But later living in New York and touring so much I had many connections to the Broadway community. I would also step into arenas that could utilize my skillset like training actors for "Avenue Q" and "The Lion King," as well as performing in Burlesque musicals like "Sugar Babies" or donating time and performances for the mega nonprofit, Broadway Cares/Equity Fights AIDS.

When one of my closest friends was auditioning as first understudy for the original cast of "Rent", she needed a gospel style song to sing. While every other black singer was doing "Amazing Grace," I pulled out the sheet music for the theme song, "Movin' On Up" from The Jefferson's. My friend was forever known for that audition. I am told the song has since been used many times by others.

In the same vein, I had several friends auditioning for Mel Brooks's "The Producers" opening on Broadway. An actor's final audition would be in front of Mel. Not only did you need a great song, it was a requirement to tell Mel a joke.

I gave one friend the song, "Mein Heir" from Cabaret. Every time she said those two words, she would point to another area of wig pieces glued to her body to reveal "Mine Hair" ... head, armpits, chest, g-string ...

I instructed another friend to sing the theme song to "The Flintstones" as a serious ballad.

And of course, I provided them with jokes that would make them seem funny when in reality ... they weren't.

Happily, all of those I helped were cast in the shows. I was living vicariously through them until I produced, "Ziegfeld's Folly: My Rise to the Middle" at the fantastic, now defunct, Zipper Theatre, home to the original production of "Hedwig and the Angry Inch." "My Rise" was one of the most important artistic and personal accomplishments of my life.

As I write this, I now recall one more Broadway connection, having a job interview when I first moved to New York. It was to be the personal assistant to one half of The Weislers. Fran and Barry Weisler have been huge, Tony© award-winning, Broadway producers for over thirty years.

"Smokey Joe's Café," "Chicago," "Rocky." The Weislers were the ones who realized, once ticket sales began to dwindle on a show, you could breathe new life into it by re-casting B,C, and D level famous or infamous celebrities. Shows extended for years thanks to Mary Lou Retton, John Secada and Donny Most. (The younger readers are thinking, "Who?" ... Exactly).

Barry was notorious for liking the ladies and Fran was just eccentric and bananas.

I remember I was escorted into Fran's office to interview for the new assistant position. I sat down and took stock of an office full of awards and photos of Fran usually wearing a glitzy dress and some sort of a wrap.

I hear someone speak, *"Hello? Hi!"*

I look around to eventually realize the voice is directed at me and coming from a speaker box on the desk.

"You're Michael, yes?"

Fran Weisler was interviewing me over the phone from her luxurious penthouse on Central Park. I imagine her laid out on a chez, in a silk robe with feather trim, coiffed, frosted hair and heels.

I'm sitting in this office alone and really not sure where to look. The meeting lasted about eight minutes, when the speaker box thanked and excused me to exit the office. It was just the weirdest thing ever. No one to hand shake, no smiles, no idea if I should shut the door or not so the box can have privacy.

Neither of us pursued a second interview.

Jackson, Culkin & 9/11

One of my specialties has always been the packaging and branding of a show, a person, or a product: the look, logo, persona, photos, slogans, art layout, and the video and audio representation in telling a story to the public.

Producer, David Gest was producing a two-night concert event celebrating Michael Jackson's thirteen years as a solo artist. It was going to be a spectacle of guest stars and production unsurpassed in the history of Madison Square Garden.

I had many friends working on the production: musicians, dancers, singers, and Emmy© nominated choreographers Glenn & Brian, today each with their own exceptional solo careers.

The boys asked me to write their bio for the concert's program, which connected me to David Gest's people who tapped me to participate in the layouts and commercial teasers for the show. It was a very small job but it allowed me some access into rehearsals, tickets to the show, and access to the after party.

I remember Michael walking into the rehearsal with what was left of his nose bandaged up. It was believed the Band-Aid was in place of a fake bridge piece he would wear during performances. When he was around the dancers, he was calm and cool. But once he'd leave the studio and have to be in the open world of hallways and larger rooms, he was like a scared bunny, dodging and darting. His pasty skin was blotched with strawberry patches not unlike Joan Rivers after leaving one of her acid peels on for too long. (See: Joan Rivers)

Cue the walk down memory lane …

In the early '90s I was working for Greg Thompson, stage producer and Guinness Book record holder who had a long running revue show at The Southampton Princess Hotel in Bermuda. It's the big pink hotel on the highest hill of the island with a gorgeous golf course.

You were treated like a guest in everyone's home when you mentioned you were in *The Follies* that ran for eighteen years on the island. I remember once a few of us stole the mini prop car used in the show, put on ski masks and ran chaos through the award-winning golf course. Security was not pleased, followed by a firm letter from the producer. *"To those responsible, please do not steal the Follies car ..."*

Michael Jackson had taken a vacation to Bermuda with his entourage and then partner in crime, Macaulay Culkin. Mac was maybe thirteen years old. (Insert dated, Jackson/boy joke here.)

Along with their luggage, they brought cases of toys to play with. When the paparazzi got too close, they would shoot water guns and balloons at them.

They all came to one of the matinee shows. Within the show there was a Motown tribute group singing "the best of." Macaulay was yelling and hopping up and down until Michael physically put him in his seat to be quiet while "the brothas" were on.

Now that I've tied in Mac, back to the main story ...

After the second night of the concert at The Garden, we went to the after party where I was approached by Mac. "Hey can you score me a Jack and Coke?" he said. I replied, "Errr, you're Macaulay Culkin. You can't get a Jack and Coke?"

Because of the fact that he had already been married and divorced, it didn't register that he was still underaged! So like the cool uncle at a wedding, I got him a double.

Wait. Didn't he become an alcoholic? Ah, well.

The Michael Jackson Concert was many things ...

It was a shocker to everyone seeing Whitney Houston rail-thin for her appearance in the show. None of the production team or cast had seen her prior because she had not attended the rehearsals. Both her and Michael's skin tones were painstakingly, digitally enhanced frame by frame in post-production.

The biggest and most current stars appeared in the concert. But my favorite part of the night was when the Jackson 5 reunited. The place went ape-shit crazy. It was electric. My guest and I, and even Lenny Kravitz behind me, simultaneously called our families and held the phone up to the sky for them to listen!

Everyone associated with this concert felt it was the jewel of their resumé and believed it would springboard their careers. But no one remembered the event.

The concert took place on September ninth and tenth, 2001. The next day, the Twin Towers came down.

Stalker #1 And Stalker #2

Let me first say that I am nobody important. I'm not famous or infamous. I'm not drop dead gorgeous and I'm not rich. So when you choose me as the one to stalk, your parents did a horrible job, you are a loser, and you should kill yourself.

I was performing at Harrah's Reno in the Sammy Davis Showroom for three months. Like many shows, we had our regular audience members and friends of the cast. Each night we would wind down at the bar and chat it up with everyone before going home. It was a fun group.

Show business people are generally very warm, touchy-feely people. So when we see someone we've met before, there is usually a hug, a kiss, or a hand-over-hand handshake. So when this kind of greeting was given to a guy I'll call "JJ," I had no idea it meant more to him than it did to me.

JJ had been employed at Harrah's for a while before quitting to work at The Bombay Company (a mall store with interior design sculptures and trinkets). So, JJ knew the cast, the staff, and later I found out, the phone extensions and security door codes. He was handsome, young, charming, and maybe a tad awkward. He'd often go out with the cast dancing or to a bar. The second time we met, he and I found ourselves casually chatting away.

But it was strange when I got a call in my hotel room from the front desk one day, telling me there was a visitor named JJ in the lobby asking if they should send him up. I didn't really recall the name since I had only met him once or twice. He came up, we chatted, there was some flirting, but it was still odd that he showed up unannounced.

Over the next few weeks, things got weirder. JJ would write

about me in his diary, photocopy it, and send the pages backstage to my dressing room. I would walk off stage, down the stairs, enter my dressing room and the phone would ring. He also sent me a gift from the sale section of The Bombay Company. It was some kind of plaster, angel wings sculpture on a post. In retrospect, I hate to interpret the angel representation. I'm heavenly? I'm dead?

Either way, folks, let me say this — Please — if you are going to stalk me, *don't send me crap.* I want the good stuff.

I had a conversation with JJ, explaining that he was a very nice person but … well, it didn't matter what came after that because all people like this hear is the "you're a very nice person" part.

One evening the cast and I went to the Harrah's cafeteria to eat between shows when I looked up to see JJ walking in. He obviously knew the pass codes to the security doors and of course knew our schedule.

While someone called security, I stood up, approached him and told him he was never to contact me again. Security escorted him out crying. I felt terrible for him, actually.

Months later, he wrote to me through my office address apologizing. He was young and eager. That's all. I remember somebody said, "Congratulations on your first stalker!" Unfortunately, it was not my last.

Many years later, I was performing in a benefit for Broadway Cares / Equity Fights AIDS. After the show we were all signing playbills out front when a young man, maybe around twenty-one or twenty-two came up alongside of me and told me he was gay but hadn't told his parents yet. In front of a few hundred people, I could only casually and quickly address him suggesting that he just follow his heart and be himself. A moment later, he tapped me on the shoulder. I turned to him. He gave me a peck on the face and ran away.

A few days later while in Europe I received an email from him and numerous emails thereafter where he let me know that he expected a close relationship of communication from me. When I didn't give it to him, he threatened to tell people I molested him.

When he saw I hadn't opened his emails or that I'd just

deleted them, he'd write disturbing things in the subject line, like one of my addresses he dug up on the Internet to prove he was coming for me. When I would reply by calling his bluff, instructing him to have his parents contact my lawyers, he'd make it sad and personal by asking, "Why don't you like me?"

After he showed up at a few performances of mine, I stopped listing the locations on my website. When I would block his emails, he would have a new address in minutes to get through to me. This went on for months. I was a basket case.

Finally, I shared this with my father over dinner. He was appalled and contacted friends in the police department who alerted the FBI, who alerted his email provider and I believe they also contacted his parents.

The messages stopped for a year before I received one final email from him. He wrote, "*Remember me?*" along with a few other disturbing comments.

The result: To this day I generally do not take photos with my arms around people or anything overly friendly, but with my hands in my pockets or behind my back.

The moral of the story? If you're gonna stalk me, save up.

The Siegfried & Roy Deal

I have had the pleasure of writing, directing, and designing many stage productions. I never think about whether the project will go further than the job at hand because, so many times, things just don't pan out. I give it my all and move on to the next job.

I developed a connection to the famed Las Vegas icons, Siegfried & Roy, through their producer, Kenneth Feld (*Disney on Ice*, *Ringing Brothers*), and later through my friendship with the handsome and talented "Voice of Magic," Darren Romeo.

In my initial, limited experience, it seemed Siegfried was the one who was kind and interested while Roy was a little more, high-strung, type A, down-to-business personality. Even in the hospital, immediately after his accident, he insisted on a note pad and pen for issuing directives! But they were both equally charming people in my company. When in conversation, either of them would put a hand on my shoulder or hold my hand to let me know I had their attention and that they appreciated those around them.

We developed a new show to franchise and extend their brand called, *Siegfried & Roy Presents*, a full scale production show around S & R's protégé, Darren. The magic team would agree to participate in the campaigns, merchandise, and licensing. We were cutting the deal with Princess Cruise Lines. This would be the first time a cruise line invested in branded entertainment.

After many months of phone conversations back and forth, I was flying to Los Angeles to meet with the head of entertainment to pound out the details. He asked for one stipulation: that neither Darren, Siegfried, nor Roy be in the room. He did not want the delicate tap dance of appeasing egos or artists during a negotiation. It was too much of a distraction that would keep him, a moneyman and bottom line corporate guy, from speaking freely. He found it stressful. The talent was not pleased to hear this but honestly, he wasn't wrong. It was agreed that, other than me, only one of them would be present in order to represent their interests.

I grabbed my suitcase for the airport and stepped into the hall to turn and lock the door, when I noticed the power was out in my building. I cursed the superintendent all the way down the nine flights of stairs. I stepped outside and saw tons of people milling about on the upper west side of a neighborhood usually quiet. This was the New York Black Out of 2003. All power was out as well as all cell phone towers.

I somehow found a payphone and credit card and called Los Angeles explaining that no one was getting out of the city. I don't know if the VP was pissed due to the inconvenience and time constraints of the decisions he had to make, or the fear of being in a room with the magician(s) by himself.

"There is no way I am having this meeting without you here," he said.

It was postponed for two weeks. Then, three days before the meeting that was to be the handshake for a long, wonderful, financially profitable deal, Roy was attacked by the tiger. Dead deal.

To be clear, S&R and the team do not believe it was an attack. Roy had a stroke, fell to the ground and the tiger grabbed him by the neck like a cub and walked him back into the holding pen where he went every night in repetition for countless years. It's true that, if the tiger wanted him dead, Roy would not be here today.

All of the cruise lines have since invested in the idea of branded entertainment: *Hairspray*, *The Second City*, *Blue Man Group*, *Dancing with the Stars*, *Nickelodeon* ...

I could name five other times in my career where I designed a potential, million dollar TV or stage concept but the timing just didn't click, there was a breach of ethics, or someone else made it happen first. You just never know! I mean, blacking out a whole city is a little extreme, but I never considered it a hint...

The King and I

Comedian, Allan King was one of the old guard ... The Catskills, The Friars, *Ed Sullivan*, *The Tonight Show* and some TV and movies. I can't say he was an A-lister, but he certainly would! As it was said many times, "*Allan's ego is bigger than his prostate.*"

I knew Allan because for many years he asked me to join The Friars Club (I have performed there many times and wrote for a few of the Roasts). I would also bump into him at Kauffman Astoria Studios in Queens, New York. He was part owner in the studios home to *Sesame Street*, *The Cosby Show* and many other programs.

I was one of several acts to perform a New Year's Eve show and Allan was the headliner.

He didn't do amazingly well compared to the rest of us, but in fairness, sometimes hype can set the bar too high for an entertainer to achieve the expected success.

After the show, a few of us were having a drink in the bar. I called Allan in his room and invited him to join us. He happily agreed. When someone like Allan King joins the group, we all know who will hold court and lead the storytelling of the evening.

On our second round of drinks, a tiny, Neil Simon-esque man bends down to the right of Allan's face and congratulates him on a good show. He then says the phrase no comic, let alone Mr. Allan King wants to hear from a civilian.

"*Mr. King, I wanted to perhaps give you one suggestion about a joke you told ...*"

The room went cold and every performer in the circle scooted their chairs away from the ticking time bomb (only psychologically of course). Allan looked straight ahead puffing on his cigar.

There was a point in Allan's show where he talks about his son telling him he has started to walk like "an old Jew." Allan demonstrates by shuffling across stage. He makes a follow up joke explaining when the Israeli army walks in a parade, the entire company shuffles down the block.

The man continues his unsolicited critique until Allan stops him without visually acknowledging the man.

Physically punctuating his sentences with the cigar, Allan begins, "You see, sir, you are already setting yourself up for embarrassment. I have been in show business for forty years. I have been a star for thirty years. So what is it that *you* are going to tell *me* about comedy?" He remains looking straight ahead, puffing away.

The man sputters, "Well Mr. King, I am Jewish and your joke about the Israeli soldiers might be construed as ..."

ALLAN
Sir! Last year I gave $400,000 to Sinai Hospital in Jerusalem!
MAN
I'm just saying that perhaps the uneducated ....
ALLAN
It's called HUMOR Sir. HUMOR.

The man looked at the rest of us for help. He was on his own. He's the one who poked the lion, he's the one who gets his ass chewed off. He tried to make a final case but with one wave of Allan's cigar, still not looking at the man, Allan said:
"You, sir, are a fool! This conversation is over!"

MAN
But I —
ALLAN
Over!

It was beautiful. I bought the next round.

Mr. Know-It-All
& The Network Show

In recent years I have written jokes for Letterman, Leno, Maher, and the Comedy Central Roasts. I co-created the MTV show *CJ and Peanut*, directed an episode of a few television shows here and there, and I have also individually coached many actors on auditions and character development. I've been able to parlay these into lectures and workshops at NYU, UCLA, the Screen Actors Guild, and at advertising and event production conventions.

I am no thespian as an actor. However, having hands on experience behind, *and* in front of the scenes for most mediums has provided me with more tricks in my bag to assist an artist in getting to where they need to be rather quickly.

I do not tell them what to do, but provide breadcrumbs or choices for an individual to choose from, so they can see how to connect the dots to the best version of their message or character (the "teach a man to fish" metaphor). This, in turn, serves all other areas of the technical production as well.

I have been approached by numerous actors who were creating a one-man cabaret show to express themselves and get away from acting like someone else or reading someone else's words. The challenge is getting them to shed their well-polished persona and to unlock the most honest version of themselves without being maudlin, in front of an intimate audience, some for the very first time in their lives.

The mistake many directors make is failing to guide performers to deeper specificity and clarity in *the actor's* writing and performance choices. You do not want to taint their voice or style with your own when participating. Of course, time is money and so whether it is stage, TV, or film, the hard part is getting them mentally prepared, quickly enough before they bankrupt the production!

Two years ago, I was called into the office of a major network to consult on a recently premiered sitcom that was tanking. After twenty minutes in the VP's office talking about the show's problems, he walked me into a conference room where I found the show's executive producer, head writer, and director. Only then did I realize they were being ambushed. I was there to tell them the bad news as a neutral party to keep the peace between the show and the network.

I decided it was important for them to realize I was not there to place blame or get someone fired. They had little time before the network would pull the plug so there was even less time for pissing contests. Everyone was clearly in an agitated state and egos needed a firm hand. I made it clear that the goal was for each person to make adjustments so their talent served everyone else.

I then explained that their biggest problem, which I knew would not be corrected by the network, was the casting. They had five second-string character actors in the group, but not one had that special something to anchor the group all together.

The second problem was that all of the actors would either play a scene at completely different performance levels and separate genres *or* they were all playing the exact same performance style. It was just all over the place, which was the director's fault.

When it's not the fault of the acting, sometimes a weak scene is due to the writing and sometimes it's the directing. You can have one stink, but not all simultaneously! Presenting new choices along with some cleaner and specific dialogue and joke stylings would give the show a breath of air and hopefully that new oxygen would unlock everything.

Once I was alone with the VP, I explained that none of this would work if I wasn't there to steer it, although at this point it didn't matter because I knew the show was going to be cancelled within the week. They had aired three episodes already and two were in the can. They simply waited too long to attempt a fix.

It's a shame. Shows are no longer allowed to grow and find their voice or their audience. The networks buy and produce over twenty pilots. Then generally only pick up three to five shows for the season. Ugly odds in a difficult business.

Two Days Turn Into
A Week With Kevin Spacey

I had no idea exactly how much of my eclectic experience I would finally get to utilize when I got a call from "Dummy Doctor," Alan Semok (ventriloquist coach to Hollywood) asking me to step in for him on a new project with Kevin Spacey.

Kevin was producing and starring in a series of short films made by young directors, one of which was called, *The Ventriloquist: Look Who's Talking*.

It's funny. Like Winona Ryder never having experienced a comedy club, Kevin seemed to have no idea that this story had been done a million times before, and I sure wasn't going to tell him. He told me while doing research he found a video of a vent online named *"Jeff Dunham?"* He never heard of the guy. Jeff isn't Kevin, but he's been around a while, right? Celebs just live in a different world than you or me.

Kevin was to play a socially awkward, sad-sack, street-performing ventriloquist, who expresses his feelings, good or bad, through his dummy. Eventually he has a breakdown, a confrontation with the dummy, and so on and so forth as seen in *Magic*, a notable episode of *Alfred Hitchcock Presents*, and when I played this similar character in David Wain's *The Ten* in 2007 opposite Winona Ryder and Paul Rudd.

Originally, I was asked to teach Kevin the technique of ventriloquism, but the production schedule was too daunting. So it was decided that during shooting, a script reader would do the dummy's lines, Kevin would manipulate the puppet's mouth then dub the voice later in post-production.

My first meeting with Kevin was at the office of his Trigger

Street Productions. He already had the dummy sent from Alan's workshop a week or so prior. I was there to teach him how to puppeteer with additional tips on the body and lip language of a ventriloquist.

I was escorted into a small studio and there was the Oscar® winner in a blue leisure suit reading the script, making notes and taking a call. He looked up, we shook hands, and I sat down to discuss things.

It was hard not to stare. He is a true thespian with an amazing body of very eclectic work. He certainly wasn't cold, but he was guarded and clearly tired.

Unlike most ventriloquists simply playing the straight man and feeding set-ups to the dummy, Kevin faced a daunting task: to be responsible for enveloping himself into a character while simultaneously manipulating the inanimate object. For many actors this would pull them out of their "personal moment" in the scene.

That was why I got a call the following day from the line producer. Kevin wanted to see me again as soon as possible, perhaps at his house in Malibu depending on our schedules. In this session I tried to show him how to best support his acting choices for the puppet as well as himself.

To coach, suggest, or support an actor in his choices is a very fine line. I did not want to come off telling him what to do. Actors are very sensitive in general, and with fame can come an additional edginess if not handled kindly.

Shooting puppets is a technically tedious undertaking; not only do you have to conceal the performers, but you have to catch the best angles along with countless other issues. Because the team had never done this before, the executive producer joined us after ten or fifteen minutes to walk them through how to perform with the puppet in order to get certain behaviors from it, how to cheat with camera tricks, and other details to prepare them for the shoot.

It was then that I realized I would need to stay on to puppeteer the dummy for the confrontation scene. So I recorded all of our sessions together to get the tempo, diction, and delivery Kevin would use for the puppet's voice. I would then learn and mimic it when shooting the scene so he could easily dub his voice over in post-production without being stuck following my style instead of his own.

I was also asked to stay and consult on production. Specifically, to go to the set and talk with the designers on how to build for puppeteer access, etc.

What began as a few days turned into almost a week of work. I was excited, honored, and confident. I was the go-to guy to make it all work. Nice to be not only an equal, but a unique one.

The day I was on location, I was brought to Kevin. We shook hands and talked about how things were going so far. He was very interested in discussing the hardships, experiments, and results in working with the puppet. We also talked about the young director and crew.

The dummy's real name was Kenny. Kenny had been given his own chair with a nameplate on it. Later that night, Kevin knocked on my adjoining trailer door and entered laughing. "Did they show this to you? You have got to see this." He showed me a miniature set of "sides" (scripts for the day's shooting) they had made for the dummy.

What I thought was funny, was that people would ask me, "Umm is the term 'dummy' okay? Should we call him Kenny?" As if I'd be offended. I said, "I don't care. I don't even know this dummy."

The documentary people also asked me to talk to them for some time about the craft, the dummy, Kevin's process, and the myriad of technical challenges.

We were interrupted when during an exterior shot, a neighboring house had a dog on the front lawn that wouldn't stop barking. On and on they tried to get a scene in the can. But the dog would not stop. Producers tried to appease the dog but to no avail. Finally Kevin got up from the set, walked across the street, up the walkway and rang the bell. A poor woman almost dropped dead to find Kevin Spacey on the other side of her door, asking if she wouldn't mind terribly bringing her dog inside for an hour or so.

The final shot of the night was the confrontation scene between Kevin and the puppet. This ventriloquist figure was an older, very standard character with moving eyes, lids, and mouth. But it was not built for the special effects or the style of performance they were asking for. I required time prior to the scene to rig the levers from the inside and out to perform it from under a table. Even then, it would be painstaking to give a clean performance. And it was.

While rigging Kenny, I told the line producer that when they shot Kevin's side of the scene, I wanted to perform the puppet's lines, not the script reader. Surprisingly, she said, "Yes, Kevin has already asked for you."

I entered the set and I immediately took the reins of support, showing Kevin where his eye line would look off camera as well as discussing the style of performance they'd want for the puppet's movements: choppy and puppet-like or more smooth and human-like. I further informed the soundman that I would need to be mic'd up so they could follow me when dubbing the audio later on (ADR). While this was a legitimate reason, I also had an ulterior motive.

On "action," the Oscar® winner went from laughing and joking with the crew, to this tortured character in one breath. I moved my puppet hand away and replaced it with my face in Kevin's line of vision. We started doing the scene. I was acting with Kevin Spacey.

We did three takes. During the reset, I walked over to the audio guy and said, "Who do I have to kill to get the mp3 recording of me and Kevin Spacey screaming at each other?" He and the photographer totally hooked me up. Of course I asked permission and kept everything to myself until after the movie release.

The last part of the shoot was filming the puppet's side of the argument. I gave them numerous takes of each line in addition to suggesting they would need head turns, eye rolls, and other cut-aways for editing. I've been around puppets my whole life so what I was doing was old hat. But to these people, when I did things like making Kenny slowly turn his head with an evil glare, everyone freaked out and clapped! When the dummy's eyelids got stuck, I adlibbed that he'd "gotten high with Spacey an hour before." The evening wrapped with clapping, laughter and sincere appreciation.

Kevin and I chatted here and there. I also carefully watched him throughout the experience. He is extremely funny and clearly very dark. He's probably a bit of a genius.

I'd like to know him socially. I'm willing to bet he plays as hard as he works.

SNL's *Saturday TV Funhouse* =
Disney Stops Calling

I had done a few voices on *Saturday Night* Live's *Saturday TV Funhouse* for creator, Robert Smigel (aka "Triumph the Insult Comic Dog") including the popular, *Ambiguously Gay Duo* (usually recording alone, it was awesome to cross schedules with Stephen Colbert one day). I also did a series of other sketches made at the expense of the corporate entity known as "Disney."

Bob was disgusted with Disney's manipulative marketing campaign telling people to hurry up and buy their movies before they "go into the vault for eighty years," forcing parents to buy them before their children's heads exploded. So the final Disney dig, spoofed that campaign with voice actors that sounded exactly like the Disney V.O. guy and numerous Disney movie characters. He also had an ex-Disney animator working on it.

There are several versions of the Mickey voice: the original, the older one I grew up with, and the current, digitally enhanced pitch that he currently has. (Yes — apparently they are still making Mickey cartoons.)

I purposely asked them not to play the reference video before I auditioned because I had no idea which voice they'd play and no man with both testicles could do the enhanced voice naturally. I did not want them to compare, instead I wanted them just to listen to me.

I was the first one to audition as Mickey Mouse and I was the one cast.

After the piece aired, I received many angry calls from the

Disney legal team. But it was out of my hands. *SNL* has a legal right to spoof without copyright prosecution and I was just a voice actor. However, for some time, I was no longer being called in for any Disney voice auditions. Totally worth it just for the story alone.

Similarly, comedian Jim Brewer and I have both been bumped from the *Fox Morning Show* hours before air, when the executive producer found that separately, we had each made a joke aimed at Republicans, in a comedy set, at some point in our lives. Lame.

About a year later, I performed the mouse one last time for the director's cut interview on a "Best Of" DVD chatting about how I (as the mouse) actually did not care much for children.

Bill Clinton Was Second On My List

Like many of the previous, high profile, high security events or productions at the Beverly Hilton, I received a call to stage manage a show.

While being a production manager or technical director puts me higher on the chain of command, when you are the stage manager, it is your template, your lead, your team, your world.

There were many times I had to step in to manage the multiple celebrity security guards, organizing and clearing the backstage area, throwing out family, friends, clients or anyone else backing Morgan Freeman into a corner or chatting Tom Cruise's ear off when he just wanted to sit down and collect himself.

There were also moments when after being informed that two of the most famous astronauts in history cannot stand one another, I had to direct wranglers to make sure their paths never crossed before getting the talent on stage.

There are two people I always wanted to meet: Oprah and President Clinton. And that week President Clinton was tentatively scheduled to participate in this very high profile, global-green fundraiser at the hotel.

The crew had been cleared two weeks prior through Secret Service as we had numerous times before for Obama, Biden, and the Royal Couple. (Will and Kate, not Barack and Joe.) We were also informed as usual that no social media leaks would be tolerated before, during, or immediately after the event. Penalty of termination and legal action would be pursued. One time Obama was coming through a back hallway of the kitchen and we were moved into a closet and locked in until he passed by.

The difficulty in managing this event would be that we had no idea when or even if President Clinton would be showing up. It would depend on his schedule that evening. So we were in contact with his handlers up to the moment prior to his entourage of vehicles making their way down Wilshire Boulevard and arriving by the hotel loading docks.

The question becomes: do you guess where in the show you will need to pause? You can't have audiences just sitting there while the emcees stretch with horrible banter. Or do you allow the President to arrive and make him wait for the right transition? Make the President wait?

Receiving confirmation eight minutes prior his arrival, I directed the deck crew to completely clear the rear and stage left. The hosts and presenters traffic would be confined to stage right. I would call certain reminders and standby cues for the ASM (assistant stage manager) while I kept the TD (technical director) and client in the loop on the headset.

Secret Service opened the back door to the theater and without skipping a beat, I firmly said, "Mr. President, I'm Michael, this way please." I did not look at him with clear vision because I did not want to be too "conscious" and stammer or ogle. I like all of our talent to feel taken care of.

I walked him to the side of the stage and gestured to an "X" on the floor. The backside of the proscenium was to his left and I book-ended him, with breathing space, on his right. There is a fine line between making someone feel secure from being bothered and exposed versus invading their space where they feel obligated to acknowledge you while trying to have a semi-private moment to compose themselves.

As he watched the CEO speak on stage I quietly explained that there was one more page of dialogue before a one-minute video would run, during which time I would walk him out to the lectern in the dark.

"Are you guys running on time tonight?" he asked.

"Actually we are ahead of schedule," I replied.

"That never happens! ... Who is this guy?" he said, pointing onstage.

"That's the CEO...He's been talking about you for five

minutes like you're friends."

Then he said the greatest, Clintonesque thing ever: "I'm everyone's friend." He grinned, knowing most people feel that way about him. It's his way. His intent. His pleasure.

The lights came down for the video. I lit the floor with a Maglite, walked him to the podium, pointed to the teleprompter, counted down from ten seconds to the end of the video, turned and exited the stage before the lights came up on him.

Afterwards he was rushed past me and out the door. I'd have killed for a photo.

27 Dresses: Heigl & Marsden

I was walking from an appointment on the Upper East Side when my agent called. A film that had already been in production for a few weeks had a role the casting directors had no luck filling. This was the final day of auditions and they would see me if I could get there before they left at 4:00 p.m. It was currently 3:05 and they were all the way downtown.

My agent sent the sides (audition script) to my phone. The role was a cab driver named "Khaleel." It was only half a page of dialogue, which I learned in the cab to the audition.

Only having one movie under my belt, I had little knowledge about character choices. Do I do an accent? Am I myself? Am I mad? Fun? Gay? I figured the director would give me direction.

The office was closing up with only a handful of people left in the room. Big fat cabbies, skinny Italian cabbies ... and one short, Jewish cabbie (me).

The audition room was tiny. I sat in a folding chair and before I read the lines I was instructed to just improv the scene. I did two takes and felt lost trying to improv with nobody in the back seat talking to me. Is it improv when you have no one to play off?

I got up, said, "Thank you," tossed the script in the trash, and walked out disgusted. I had no idea what I was doing. I'm certainly no actor. An hour later I got the call that I had booked the role.

The money for a job like this is average for a non-celebrity. But it is the residual checks that really add up to make a difference and once in a while, cover your ass when work is tight.

The residual checks come in waves, each representing maybe six to ten months.

The original release in the US

The international release

The US DVD release

The international DVD release

The reruns

Ancillary venues (planes, ships, hotels)

As the years go by, the amount trails off. Just yesterday, I got a check from NBC for thirty-seven cents.

But major movie residuals are *amazing*.

Back to the movie ...

The original one page of dialogue turned into quite a few more after my improvised audition. We shot my segments for a week. Unfortunately, as in my first film, most of the performance went on the cutting room floor and did not re-appear in the DVD! I thought I did some funny stuff.

They did, however, place me in the first ten minutes and the last ten minutes, bookending the film. It made the part seem bigger than it was for a co-star listing. By the way, the part they kept in the middle where I threw the shoes at Katherine Heigl was not in the script. I just wanted to see her run for it.

Like most actors, I spent much of my time waiting in my trailer. The rest of the time was spent sitting in the taxi with no a/c in the middle of a heat wave. You can't use air conditioning when recording sound. You also can't sweat when recording images.

Choreographer turned director, Anne Fletcher and I bonded over family, comedy, and mutual friends in the movie, *Hairspray*. She was strong, beautiful, and still had the heart and playfulness of the giddy, loving beings called "dancers" that I've been around since I was sixteen.

Without any coaching, she started calling me "Ziggy," my nickname since I was a kid. It almost felt like a brother/sister-like comfort and by day two everyone started calling me by my nickname.

The closing credits list my character as "Khaleel" but Katie (That's right, I called Katherine Heigl, Katie.) called me Ziggy a few times in the film. It was an accident. But I always joked that

I was such a poor actor, they had to call me by my actual name or I would never know when to respond.

Anne told me the cab driver could be played to the level of the *Seinfeld* character, Kramer. After watching scenes between Katherine and James Marsden, it just felt out of place to play the character that way. I knew it didn't match and I had no barometer to know how to make that choice work for me. I also knew that on film you move with minimalism because when your face is ten feet high on a screen it's easy to look crazy. So I played it straight. No thespian here.

During the week together in a cab all alone (the real cab or the fake cab on the tow truck where, if I actually touched the wheel or brakes I'd overturn the whole thing), Katherine was very funny. I was already told she liked improv and goofing around.

When the director asked me to pull in the cab for the eleventh time, I looked at Katherine and yelled, "I'm giving 'em gold here!" She tried to yank my chain by telling me to step it up when I replied, "Hey! I am clearly carrying you throughout this entire film!"

I also told her that *Grey's Anatomy* was doing a lot of gyno stories lately and I was tired of it. She chimed in revealing the writers come up with countless alternatives to the word "vagina," a word used excessively for some reason. I made her give me examples. We were so giddy from the heat we somehow started singing the Justin Timberlake/SNL hit, "Dick in the Box."

"I should introduce you to my friend TR." She suggested a set-up with TR Knight. I was in a relationship at the time so that couldn't happen, but this movie gave me major points with my guy thanks to co-star James Marsden.

The guy I was seeing at the time (I'll call him "Mark") loved *X-Men* and of course James played "Cyclops." James also played "Corny Collins" in the movie, *Hairspray*, which was released during the shooting of our movie.

I explained to James that Mark was a Broadway performer who was going to be singing backup for him when he and the movie cast of *Hairspray* performed on *The Today Show* that Friday. So when I asked him if he wouldn't mind saying hello to

Mark when he came to the set, he said, "Of course."

When Mark visited me on the set, I walked him to James's chair, introduced them and left them to chat for a while. But that wasn't the end of the major points I earned. That Friday when Mark stood with the ensemble at *The Today Show* broadcast, heartthrob James Marsden entered, walked over to Mark, gave him a big hello and a huge hug in front of all of Mark's peers. BAM! WHO'S THE KING? I AM! I milked that for a week.

In recent years, Katherine Heigl has gotten a label of being difficult. Only once do I recall her "stomping her foot." But in all fairness it was the last shot of the film and we were running very late.

When I got to the set the first day, I was warned to not engage Katherine's mother, who was also her manager. I was told she was difficult and not nice. It was clear she was keeping her daughter on a pedestaled path to the Academy Awards and everyone would treat her star daughter *as* a star.

Katherine had expressed interest in visiting the Jim Henson Studio lot and we made tentative plans for the following week when we would both be back in LA. She was also bringing TR.

I was sitting in my chair having touch ups applied. Katherine's mother was next to me knitting or crocheting something that clearly kept her completely closed off emotionally. And being me, I turned to her and reiterated our plans for next Thursday and invited her along. She looked at me over her glasses and said, "She won't have time for that." And then turned back to her crocheting. (Excuse me. Is that a soul you're darning?)

I'm hoping the problem has been the mother. Katherine was a brassy, fun lady. I enjoyed her.

I have had bigger roles in my career. But the exposure from this tiny role in a big studio, chick-flick movie had people recognizing this small-time performer. Girls would get giggly and ask for photos for months. It was really fun. On the creative checklist, I was pleased to have the experience.

For a while after, I kept getting requests to audition for cab driver roles. I could see the future of my career..."Hi, I'm Michael Paul Ziegfeld. You might remember me as the cab driver in...everything I've ever done."

The Party's Over

When I'm asked after I perform, "How was the show?" by friends or co-workers, I find it's not an easy question to answer. A good show for the audience that evening may not be anything special for me. Or vice versa. But sometimes there's a show where I, the techs, the venue, the schedules, the time, the weather, and the audience are in alignment. It's like everyone whistling in the same key. The material anchors the show with symbiotic, organic, spontaneous, multi-layered improvisation. There is a very carefully slight filter on the brain to execute narratives that instigate roaring walls of laughter and clapping and yelling back and forth with the audience. There are times where I almost don't want to leave the stage. It's nice to know it still exists for me ... and for them.

About eight years ago I cut my workload down to explore other areas of the business, specifically writing and directing. I cut my bookings in half to be in town and available. Over all, I was able to pick and choose gigs, timeframes and money. But after the economy tanked, my booking options were starting to decline dramatically. I started thinking maybe I was losing my touch. Maybe my material and brand was dated.

I wrote new material, repackaged myself, and went back to find the venues and outlets from the highest point of my career. What I found was that while I was taking a break, those venues disappeared. Celebrities weren't paying for opening acts to tour anymore. Clubs were paying almost nothing with sixteen "comics" (I use the term loosely) on the roster, each doing six minutes. Who can create an arc and bond with an audience in six minutes? Not me. And the casinos were sinking their money into *Cirque du Soleil* shows.

Eventually my most consistent calls were from the cruise ship industry. For years I played the biggest rooms with the biggest names. Now my mother's friends introduced me with the tag, "*He performs on cruise ships!*" I hated it.

Don't get me wrong, work is work and I am pleased to be wanted. I will always give one-hundred and ten percent and I understand how to make that venue work.

It took a few jobs to understand that these were probably the hardest audiences to play to, consisting of every age, size, and religion in the same room. It was a vast demographic of people who hadn't paid to come see me, so their incentive to enjoy my performance was nil, leaving me with the task of winning their respect (or in some cases, beating them into submission).

The big problem was many of the cruise lines tend to make it very difficult to succeed by running their shows like just another corporate program. It is definitely not show business. It is entertainment.

And while they do a lot of big talk regarding quality and high standards, the cruise ships are generally summer camp for adults and the staff are generally the camp counselors. A lot of things fall through the cracks and the performer is left responsible to try and succeed. Of course if we don't, we don't get asked back.

At a certain point in your career, you just want to look at the kids in the tech booth or the entertainment directors that were the food and beverage managers six months ago and say, "It's my twenty-fifth year. Shut the fuck up and just do what I say."

The cruise ships have always had a negative stigma in show business primarily because years ago they were filled with cheesy, lounge lizard acts with fake credits and less talent. Or is that less credits and fake talent...?

While that may still be somewhat of a factor, there is also some quality work being done out there with theaters built as well or better than Broadway houses. The money can be very good and many "name" performers are sneaking around out there doing shows because "the road" isn't what it once was.

But the truth is, they make it too hard to get the job done

anymore. So I'm winding things down. Anyway, I don't want to be eighty years old, alone, staring at a wall of career photos. I want other things now.

Of course when I tried to quit the first time in the late '90s, I wrote a new bit for my final gig and I was awarded Atlantic City's Act of the Year.

This time, the minute I was ready to walk away, calls came in again ... a holding deal with NBC/Universal, a new agency, this book. But I have resolve this time around. I'm ready.

I will miss sitting in a dark, air conditioned theater tech-ing lights and sound. I will miss the roar of the crowd on a really good night. I will miss the bonding sessions and storytelling with those who share this exclusive experience. I will miss the artistry.

I've worked for myself since I was eighteen. It's been a good, tough run. I'm ready to not be the boss anymore. I'm ready to check my mailbox daily and enjoy my couch. I'm ready for a warm, full social life with roots. I'm ready to do my craft in my spare time because I *want* to, not because I *need* it to pay my bills. I also never want to pack another suitcase ever again. *Maybe*, a lunch bag.

To the producers, directors, agents, writers, technicians, cirque performers, impressionists, comics, magicians, jugglers, ventriloquists, dancers, singers, actors, puppeteers, travel agents, drivers, dressers, assistants, PR reps and hospitality hosts...thanks for the work, friendship, respect, and support.

The first half of my life will provide amazing stories for my children ... that is if I meet someone ... and get married ... and have kids. Although my swimmers are probably a little retarded at this point, so adoption might be best. Or I'll just get a plant.

I'm gonna go do something else now, and maybe stop talking for a few years.

Thanks,
Michael Paul Ziegfeld

PS: I'm looking for a job. So, if you know of anything ...

A Few Published Comedic Editorials

"Excessive Clapping Along And The 'Round Of Applause'"
By Michael Paul Ziegfeld

I am finally coming out against the stage performer's abuse of the request for us, the audience, to "clap along." We don't *want* to clap along. I'm off, you're working, I paid for this ticket, *you* clap along. Clapping along should come from me being inspired enough in whatever you're doing to want to clap along.

But once I do give in to clapping along (usually out of public pressure), how long do I have to clap along for? The entire song? Until the performer stops clapping along? I feel uncomfortable stopping before the person next to me for fear of being judged that I am an unappreciative audience member. I am appreciative of the performance, just not the request and responsibility laid upon me to clap along. It's the equivalent of having to do the YMCA hand gestures so the bar-mitzvah band leader doesn't feel alone and lame.

Asking me to clap along more than once in the show makes my hands hurt. Maybe I clap too hard. But what if one's clap doesn't make a lot of noise? Or any? Sometimes if my hands are too dry, I clap along and nothing comes out. But when the performer can see me, I clap anyway ... I panto-clap.

This also goes for the request to give someone a "round of applause" ... a guest musician, an assistant, an audience member. Rounds of applause are requested for the entrance, the exit or an additional "good job" reinforcement because, "They can hear ya backstage! Go ahead and give them another round of applause!" They can't hear us backstage. They're already in the dressing room, in the car or on the phone ripping someone to shreds.

Performers beat this to death generally because they are lazy self-show directors and want to fill the transitional silence. Tell me who's coming to the stage. If I am excited about the surprise, I'll happily give a round of applause before they even do anything, as I am expected to do. If I am inspired by their performance, I will give a big one when they leave to say thanks ... unless I'm applauding because I am happy they are finished and leaving.

When I bring three audience members up on stage for one of my closing bits, I ask a little about them to make them feel comfortable, then I say to the audience, "Thank them for joining us for the big finish!" thereby getting into the bit. Ya, it's the same thing and I could get away with not doing it at all, but it feels different! It's like the difference between asking a child to kiss his grandma or telling him to. Only at the end, after a job well done, I ask for the round of applause for these unwilling participants as they exit, in place of giving them a parting gift like a free DVD that I sell in the gift shop (or online at www.michaelpaulonline.com).

There are other exceptions to this rule. It is one thing if you are sharing the stage with, let's say, the band. You are acknowledging other artists. *But* if you acknowledge the musician every time there's a solo in every other song, then no. I'm tired and I would like a round of applause for my participation too. For the record, nothing is worse than a performer asking us to give ourselves a round of applause. Now I have to applaud for you, the guest and myself? No. Go be a program director at a retirement village and lead a session of karaoke.

As for stopping the whole show to introduce the stage crew...stop doing this. The reason the lighting, sound, and stage techs work backstage in the dark is so they are not seen. They know the gig. They wear all black to blend in! It is their job to create a mood in your show that is natural and subliminal for our audience experience. You don't peel the covers back to reveal the bed bugs and this isn't your high school production of *Damn Yankees*. I was a tech for many years. Just thank us privately with liquor, food, or cash and skip the round of applause.

*****

Our Next Topic: When watching *Saturday Night Live* or any late night talk show monologue, at what point did we replace laughing after a joke with the pacifying gesture of whoo-ing and clapping? If you are whoo-ing and clapping, it's because you didn't think it was funny enough to laugh. Stop robbing the performer of his responsibility, no matter what the audience warm-up guy tells you!

*****

"What I Expect From My Homeless"
By Michael Paul Ziegfeld

Years ago, I remember meeting friends in Philadelphia's University City. I gave a homeless person money. When I exited the restaurant an hour later, I saw him jump into a Cadillac with his other friends, counting the cash. I felt angry and robbed. A friend said that my intention was the important thing. But I am no longer a fan of handing money over to people on the street. However, there are always exceptions.

In New York City, the homeless are fun and very talented. The Motown group, the mariachi band, the break dancers whose big closer is a three-year old dressed like them ... Sure there's the occasional a cappella soloist singing "I believe the children are our future" ... in which case I offer them a dollar to stop singing. I figure it's not gonna make me any more rich or poor and it's a community service against noise pollution.

But don't expect me to give anything to you just because you gave an unsolicited performance. I was perfectly fine having a quiet subway ride. I gave money to the Motown singers and was then berated by another homeless man. "Why the f**k do they get money and I don't!" he yells. "Because they didn't shake a cup in my face that's why!" I reply.

For better or worse I've been desensitized to the homeless people that scour the city in Los Angeles. Some talk, argue, and even get into physical altercations with themselves. In LA, the homeless are crazy and they'll kill ya.

I find whether you are helping them or not, if you don't ignore them and address them directly, no harm will come to you. They know you see them, so acknowledge them. I can be direct, respectful and still say "no" with personal strength so they don't mess with me. Approached first thing in the morning I've cut them off, with one hand up stating, "It's too early for this!" After hustling all day I've replied, "You're askin' the wrong guy buddy. I got no work comin' in." At a stoplight by the tranny-hooker-donut shop I'll say, "I like your dress man-lady!"

Some homeless look perfectly healthy and even dress well. People, if you're gonna play the homeless card, do not wear your new high-tops or tweed jacket. Simply messing up your hair does not sell the product.

Props are generally lame too. How do some guys own a dog but don't own a home? I've had a dog. They are damn expensive. Showing me your dog and telling me you're hungry? You should eat your dog. Man's best friend can be man's best meal. Don't be picky. You're homeless.

Some aren't homeless, they're just asking for money. To you panhandlers: Don't be lazy and unprepared. Have an act. I'm a comic. You probably already have more money than I do.

Have you seen the young black boys who have huge boxes of M&Ms they're selling for their basketball team? It's November. There is no basketball now. And why do you have to start the announcement with *"Ladies and gentlemen, I am not doing drugs or stealing ..."* Hey guy — the homeless start that same sentence when they ask for handouts. It's plagiarism and a disjointed logic to boot. *"HEY! I'm not a Nazi and I don't have crabs! Give me a dollar!"* You never heard Ron Popeil start off that way before pitching "The Juicer."

There's a little Chinese lady who sells nothing but those pencil top "Whirlies." I don't know what it's really called but it's a piece of neon green plastic that sits on top of a pencil. It lights up and makes a whirly sound when you shake it vigorously. Has anyone in the last twenty years seen her shuffle through the train and thought to themselves, "*Ya know? I need that.*" She sells one every six months. Does she go home to her family bragging about her sales technique? She's probably far more successful than her brother-in-law who stood at the exit to the Lincoln Tunnel all day holding one, five dollar bouquet of flowers that he couldn't sell.

Somehow I find her "job" more annoying or insulting than being homeless and asking for a handout. She is enabling the production of crappy toys and getting mindless people to buy them, polluting our planet with more garbage. That being said, I believe there were only fifty-two "Whirlies" produced and they are just circulated around the world along with fruitcakes and Caribbean pirate coconut heads.

I do love the Cybil-esque switcheroo for the homeless that praise you to Jesus while asking for money until you snub them. Then they curse you to the fiery depths of hell.

Life is hard. I'm killin' myself to make it. So sometimes I just want to give and get honesty from my fellow man. When I don't, well, it generally goes something like this ...

Walking Out of the Subway

Homeless Woman: "Jesus loves you. Can you spare me some money?"

Me: "No, sorry."

Homeless Woman: "Well why the hell not, cracker-ass ?"

Me: "Because I am one paycheck away from not paying my rent and I'm out workin' my ass off. What are *you* doin?"

Homeless Woman: "We'll, that's all you had to say!"

Me: "Well, that's what I *did* say!"

Homeless Woman: "Okay!"

Me: "Okay!"

In Penn Station

Pan Handler: "Scuze me. I'm not looking for a hand out, but I'm taking a train to Harrisburg and it's twelve dollars and I only have seven."

Me: "Okay ... so what can I do for you?"

Pan Handler: "Well, I'm not looking for anything. I'm just saying you know, I'm taking this trip to Harrisburg and the ticket is twelve dollars."

Me: "Right? So what are you asking me?"

Pan Handler: "Well I'm just asking for some Christian brotherhood, you faggot m*therf**ker!"

Me: "Hmmm, okay well, number one, you should have just said what you wanted instead of this tap dancing around, and, number two, I don't think you can use the term "Christian brotherhood" and "faggot m*therf**ker" in the same sentence.

So basically here's what I'm looking for from my homeless.

Show a real skill, an act, a talent.

Get to the point.

Learn the full lyrics to "Greatest Love." It's been done. At least do it well and have some kind of instrumental.

* * *

"Speaking Out Against The General Public's Usage Of The Verbal Rim Shot"
By Michael Paul Ziegfeld

It's hard to remember before the '90s when stand-up comedy had yet to be on every television channel or on every street corner establishment holding a comedy night. You had to search it out in record stores, Vegas, and a few small clubs. But since then, it's become as nonchalant as Starbuck's or homeless tranny hookers.

The comedians have also been desensitized. Comics used to dress up and it was mostly men doing it. Now you're lucky if the person showered before the show or is wearing pants, and it is unclear as to whether the performer you just watched is male, female, or "other." None of this is negative or positive. Except for one item I take issue with.

Over the last twenty years there have been certain comedic stock lines that have joined the spoken word of the civilian or "audience" as you, the general public, might call yourselves. You might recognize: "Try the veal," "Drive safely," or the "badum-bum" (i.e. the verbal rim shot).

In vaudeville and burlesque, performers used the verbal rim shot as a positive acknowledgement of where the joke or line had humorously taken the audience. It was a comedic punctuation, if you will.

However, the public has made it a weak, flabby punch line with less depth than a Miley Cyrus song without understanding the history and dimensions of its usage. If "supercalifragilisticexpialidocious" were used in the same manner, no one would care about Mary Poppins's talking umbrella one bit! (Okay, that was the worst analogy ever.)

Allow me to educate you.

On or off stage, as a tag line or in conversation, the verbal rim shot was used by our comedic, ancestral industry professionals the way Jewish elders spoke Yiddish. Both are a slang language with a vocabulary that is less about definition but more described by feelings and situations. The words can also share multiple meanings depending on those situations and the people involved.

To this day, comedians use the "badum-bum" in a spectrum of ways...laughter and excitement, or tongue-in-cheek, or as an inside joke revealed to the audience. It has layers of underlying meanings to it which include anything from the journey it took to write the line, the appreciation to the other comic for his or her contribution to the bit within their conversation, or an understanding of the pain they all are subjected to when the joke falls flat and why. But with any of those reasons, it is always from a positive, warm, productive place...a place of community and safety and joint responsibility and protection...a place that you, the general public have not paid dues for.

When a joke is made by one regular person to another, replying with the "badum-bum" is negative. It is shutting the person down. It has the connotation that the innocent joke or repartee was schlocky, hacky, or just plain lame. It lowers one person and raises another. And humor should never be doused, especially the innocent expression of one's humor coming out naturally. It is playful and kind. Isn't it nice that someone is expressing himself or herself in an attempt to connect with other human beings without hate?

Well, comedians hate you for doing it. And doing it to a comedian is the rudest, most insulting thing a civilian could do. It's like a non-Marine yelling, "hooyah!" Or doing the secret handshake to a Mason lodge member. Ya weren't in the war and you don't wear a fez so you can't use our stuff.

My friend Mary contends that the rim shot was being done in conversation by her grandfather years before I was born! Well that doesn't mean it's right!

Only weeks ago she told me the word "retarded" was used by medical practitioners years ago because science had yet to discover and dissect the origin of individual diseases. Once they learned better, they changed their vocabulary. In which case, the "badum-bum" should stop being used now that people realize they are using it in random and often derogatory contexts!

A white man cannot use the "n-word." But it's fine for black people to use it with each other. In turn, the verbal rim shot is only for comics, comedic acts and writers. It is for internal usage only.

The power of the "badum-bum" should be used for good, not evil and cannot be left in the hands of novices. Not to mention the fact that once something comes into America's mainstream vernacular, an irresponsible public usually pummels and squeezes it for every bit of life it has before throwing it away, lifeless and washed up, like Melanie Griffith.

So like the Hobbit's ring, Arthur's sword, or Flava Flav's clock necklace, I am spearheading the movement to take the verbal rim shot back to the safe and responsible hands of its masters, the comedic performers.

Critics And Clients

"Really funny and obviously a good writer." — Jimmy Brogan, Head Writer - *The Tonight Show with Jay Leno*

"We knew he was one of the best comedians working. We were lucky to get him." — David Wain, Director - *The Ten*

"Funny stuff and well played by Heigl and the cabdriver, Michael Ziegfeld, who both make the most of the slapstick possibilities." — *E Talk Hollywood*

"... Such a pro and so fun to work with. The pleasure was all ours!" — Carter Swan, Executive Producer - Trigger Street Productions

"... Precise and nuanced. That short scene demonstrates just about the most perfect manipulation I've ever seen." — Alan Semok, Film & Television FX Master

... A comedian with serious acting chops!" — Jonathan Stern, Executive Producer - *Children's Hospital*/City Lights Pictures

"He was fantastic. I've given raves and blessings on him." — Dusty Bennett, Disney Broadway Theatrical Productions

"With his technical craftsmanship and clever script, he is the most impressive voice-thrower to hit the showroom stage in many years ... a spicy, winning performance!" — Chuck Darrow, *Courier Post* - Atlantic City

"He has certainly made a lot of new fans since his arrival...." — Bob Dee, *Fun & Gaming Magazine* - Reno/Tahoe

"He sends audiences into an uproarious frenzy!" — Lori Beth Sussman, *Jackpot Magazine* - Gulf Coast

"He's the perfect blend of talent...warm, friendly and delightfully funny!" — John Kravitz, NBC - Atlantic City

"We laughed our heads off. Absolutely brilliant!" — Caroline Hunt, Richmond Television Syndication

"He wouldn't let the audience breathe! They were holding their stomachs from laughter pains." — Darren Romeo, Siegfried & Roy Productions

"Ziegfeld bandies with the audience so well!" — Mel Shields, *Showtime Magazine* - Nevada

"He has great range!" — Cathy Lizzio, CED Agency

"Michael is a virtual whirlwind of talent!" — Nancy Glass, Anchor - *American Journal*

"You rarely see such showmanship anymore...he's just wonderful!" — The Amazing Kreskin

"He's got something that audiences welcome, charm & talent!" — Arthur Novell, Celebrity Publicist - Markham/Novell LTD.

"He's so multifaceted because he has really studied the business." — Greg Thompson, Guinness World Record Stage Producer

"Besides being hilarious, he has a great voice, character acting skills and even made me tear up at times." — Evie Aronson, *Last Comic Standing*

"My work as a cartoonist and national journalist for CBS News has made me realize the importance of Michael's skills. Understanding an audience is key, as is communicating with them and entertaining them. He has a depth of knowledge in many areas, including comedy, directing, writing, presenting information, audience dynamics, and much more. His impressive experience and skill set are only the beginning. He also has the skill of explaining skills.

I have also worked with Michael on production teams where I find him professional, punctual and reliable. On a personal note, his conscientiousness is matched by his kindness and thoughtfulness. He is a friend to many, with a way of remembering what is special to people." — Mitch Butler, Journalist — CBS NEWS

"Michael Paul is our go to when we are looking for someone to manage difficult or sensitive clients and oversee production on our large scale events. We produce over 300 award style events and corporate meetings a year and are grateful to have him on our call list." - Rachel Wolfe, Director – ENCORE EVENT TECHNOLOGIES

"Working with a director on a cabaret wasn't something I'd ever considered doing. I find the medium extremely personal. However, when I finally decided to take that step Michael was able to help me clarify story points and step out of myself in a way that made my show more successful than I ever could have imagined. His help was a great way to take my live shows to their next level." — Jai Rodriguez, Actor - *Queer Eye*, *Malibu Country*, and *Rent*

"I first met him in 2001 when he stepped in last minute to technically design a concert that moved the audience by marrying the look to the sound. What resulted was a performance that led artist, Shayna Steele to a record deal, several recordings and eventually gigs around the world.

I had once seen his variety show. He had the audience in the palm of his hand for the entire hour, and it was a treat to see someone with such attention to detail and love of craft. There are quite a few things in common between jazz musicians and comedians: always trying to be ahead of the curve, total and complete immersion in the scene, ability to improvise or simply execute rehearsed material — and I have constantly been impressed with Michael in all of these regards. His clients will benefit immensely." — David Cook, Jazz Keyboardist/Musical Director for Taylor Swift, Natasha Beddingfield, Jennifer Hudson, 'N SYNC

"I first met MPZ while at Comedy Central in 2003. Michael receives the call for help from multiple mediums because he has truly studied the business. In an age where people must wear multiple hats to compete for employment, he has an encyclopedia of information providing a fluid, unique, diverse sensibility." — Tony Colon, VP of Production - Unscripted Programming

"I've had the opportunity to use his "Show Doctor" talents to add more comedy and direction to a script that had already been through the edits of more than a few comedy writers. In one day, he brought in fresh ideas and very useable material that took the script up a few notches immediately. Insightful notes on characters, pacing, structure, and other theatrical elements came with his work as well. He knew what the strengths were and how to play them up. Never straying from the original vision of the show by keeping all the comedic material in context.

Communication is always done with professionalism and respect. Collaboration with Michael is smooth and notes are presented with direct, honest comments. His goal is always to improve the final result.

Michael knows the craft of building shows. He has both the ability to make a marketable product and how to sell that product. He is always responding immediately to emails & phone calls, clearly setting goals to achieve, achieving them, and dealing with the business side with skill equal to his artistic and creative flair.

Anyone who has the pleasure of working with this talented

and experienced performer, creator, director, writer, technician, and businessman will always return for a second helping. I know of no one else that can bring so much to the table as Michael Paul Ziegfeld." — Charles Bach, International Illusionist

"Michael's process for preparing quickly for a scene is dead on. In a very short time, my videotaped, television audition scenes had arc, movement and a depth I had never achieved so quickly. When all was said and done, my agent, who NEVER says anything, wrote back and said, "Fantastic audition!" Besides being a great friend, and fantastic performer himself, I now count Michael as my incredible acting coach." — Jeri Sager, Broadway Actress - *Les Miserables*, *Cats*, *Sunset Boulevard*

"I am acutely aware of someone's abilities to teach others, to 'get the job accomplished,' and maintain a high regard for technical precision and production values.

Michael Paul has all of these abilities. He has an immense knowledge of stage and theater, with a vast spectrum of twenty-five years experience in the entertainment and hospitality industry. He is able to work with any type of person and personality, from stagehand to top headliner, with finesse and grace. He is an asset to any organization." — Bobbi Taylor, Coordinator - Trump Entertainment

About the Author

You might remember him from The Tonight Show, Sex and the City, Family Physician, Sesame Street, The Ten co-starring with Winona Ryder or 27 Dresses opposite Katherine Heigl, voicing and puppeteering for Jim Henson Productions, Saturday Night Live, Dick Clark, MTV, VH-1, Walt Disney Productions, and numerous national commercial campaigns. He has opened for or split the bill with Lewis Black, Joan Rivers, Lisa Lampanelli, Margaret Cho, Jeff Foxworthy, Rita Rudner, Phyllis Diller, Brett Butler, Wynonna Judd, James Brown, The Pointer Sisters, The Beach Boys, Kenny Rogers, Norm Crosby and The Mills Brothers. He's had an audience with Her Royal Majesty, Queen Elizabeth II, and Atlantic City Magazine has named him Act of the Year. He has written for Real Time with Bill Maher, The Late Show, The Friar's Roasts, editorials for The Huffington Post, stand-ups, actors & CEOs and consulted or directed for Kevin Spacey, CBS Scripted and numerous theatrical and cabaret productions.

Web: **http://www.michaelpaulonline.com**
Twitter: **@MichaelPaulLive**
Facebook: **https://www.facebook.com/MichaelPaulOnline**
Instagram: **MichaelPaulOnline**